Doggerel

THE MOVING MEMOIRS OF RESCUE DOGS
AND THEIR SECOND LIVES

In poetry and prose

ANGELA PATMORE

Spring Hill

DEDICATION

To the dog charities, shelter staff and rescue workers and to my dear dog Jo

Published by Spring Hill, an imprint of How To Books Ltd,
Spring Hill House, Spring Hill Road,
Begbroke, Oxford OX5 1RX
Tel: (01865) 375794
Fax: (01865) 379162
info@howtobooks.co.uk
www.howtobooks.co.uk

The paper used for this book is FSC certified and totally chlorine-free. FSC (The Forest
Stewardship Council) is an international network to promote responsible management of
world's forests.

The right of Angela Patmore to be identified as authors of this work has been asserted by her
in accordance with the Copyright, Designs and Patents Act 1988.

Text © 2010 Angela Patmore
Cover illustration © 2010 Natalie Mascall
Illustrations by David Mostyn
British Library Cataloguing in Publication Data
A catalogue record for this book is available from the British Library

ISBN 978-1-905862-58-0

Produced for How To Books by Deer Park Productions, Tavistock, Devon
Designed and typeset by Baseline Arts Ltd, Oxford
Printed and bound in Slovenia on behalf of Latitude Press Ltd

NOTE: The material contained in this book is set out in good faith for general guidance and
no liability can be accepted for loss or expense incurred as a result of relying in particular
circumstances on statements made in the book. The laws and regulations are complex and
liable to change, and readers should check the current position with the relevant authorities
before making personal arrangements.

CONTENTS

ACKNOWLEDGEMENTS

I should very much like to thank all the owners who allowed their beloved dogs to be versified in this book. I should also like to thank the following:

Joanna Lumley

Bel Mooney

Annette Crosbie OBE

BBC Wildlife Artist of the Year Natalie Mascall for allowing us to use her portrait of Bracken Hilling on the front cover

Ivor Stocker and the Retired Greyhound Trust

Clarissa Baldwin and the staff of Dogs Trust

Sara Wilde, James Skinner and the Kennel Club

Anne Carter and the Labrador Lifeline Trust

Robin Allison-Smith for his photograph of Bonnie, the Maltese Dog

Peter Corns for use of his photograph of Jasmine

Tessa Codrington for her photograph of Otto

Jon and Anne Hunt, Keith and Margaret Miller, Dorothy and David Burder and Maureen Percival for their tireless help with research

And finally...
publishers, Giles Lewis and Nikki Read, for believing in the project

Foreword by JOANNA LUMLEY

It seems very dreadful that the more we become aware of the wretchedness of abandoned dogs, the more frequently they are cruelly treated and discarded, sometimes for simply behaving like the dogs they are.

Angela Patmore's enchanting book has burrowed into the minds of our most loyal friends; her poems are touching, humorous and revealing (I suspect she may have canine genes in her make-up). There are case histories here to jag at your heart, to make you almost ashamed to be human: but the overall impact is of redemption, of wrongs made right by adoption by kind new owners. In her words, in the poem Zak, "....A dog can reform. A dog can learn. A dog can be reborn."

Rescue dogs are often the most rewarding of friends as they are so grateful to have a loving home. They want to please us so that we won't throw them out again. There is usually a reason for a dog being difficult, and it's often man-made. They can be reborn as a good dog with time and care and love. Above all, she captures the entirely different characters and natures of the animals she writes about, because anyone who owns and loves an animal knows that no two are the same, any more than people are.

If I had a wish I would choose to be able to talk to the animals like Doctor Doolittle. I wish I knew what they think of us and why they continue to long for our company. The poet Henry Beston wrote: " They are not underlings; they are other nations, caught with ourselves in the net of life and time, fellow prisoners of the splendour and travail of the earth." Maybe by treating animals better we shall ourselves become finer people. After all, a nation is judged by the way it treats its animals. By buying this book you will be helping to unite unwanted animals with the new lives they deserve, loved by new owners, their painful past healed over and forgotten.

And perhaps you will even think of adopting a dog yourself: a greater treat I cannot imagine.

PART ONE

The Poems

Alice

Little Alice, still unsure
Was kept in the dark in a shed.
She had no bowl and she had no bed
And little he cared if she were dead
As he threw her food in the door.

Little Alice was going grey,
Hopes fading out of her head.
But somebody heard of the life she led
And, grabbing her fast before she fled
Carried that girl away.

Little Alice, now safe and sound,
Has eyes that are button bright.
Her face turned white to give her some light
But she's curious, cute and quite all right
A great little grey greyhound.

Alice was born on 9th September 1998. She had spent the first three years of her life in a shed and was very nervous and shy when Cindy and Tony Hilling acquired her from one of the Retired Greyhound Trust branches for whom Cindy works as a home checker. Now Alice is thriving. She shares Cindy and Tony's Essex home with lurcher Bracken and twelve other beloved rescue greyhounds – many of them, like Alice, the victims of past cruelty.

Alvin

Bundle of nerves and desperate to please:
Dumped on a Portsmouth street.
Squirmed in a small cage for a year.
Scar on his lip, and limps a bit.
Humans have been hard on his breed.
What did these ones need, or fear?
Should he look fierce, fight, compete?
Or should he give these his love?
If he guessed right they might take him along.
If not, like thousands more
He'd go through that trap door
Where all the Staffies go

Who try to please and just guess wrong.
We took him for a long walk on the lead:
Noticed some crossing to avoid him.
Alvin the joyous, keen to meet and greet.
First night in the dark, snuffled and peed.
Searched under our king-size bed.
We felt the earth move – that was Alvin's head
Shifting the weight. Still, 'from the strong
Cometh forth sweetness' – and an apelike song:
Mewlings and strange growlings.
Yet when the carol singers came
Feeling utterly out of his depth
Alvin wet himself on our step.
Up for a bundle with the lads,
Gentle with women, kind to kids.
Sitting oddly on his bum
Crossing his bandy legs –The Geezer –
Belly protruding like a beery tum:
Look at our Monkey – made of sterling stuff
Loyal and loving. We'd have fifty like him.
Give them a chance, this breed so feared, derided:
Could be those anti–Alvins are misguided.

*In November 2009 Lorraine and Peter Eyles visited Albery Dog
Rescue in Bedfordshire run by an ex-vet called Joy. Among the dogs
they saw, recalls Lorraine, was 'a very anxious' Alvin. 'We had had
no experience with a strong-willed bull terrier, but he was a very
stable, friendly, curious little chap. He gets on well with other dogs
and has many girlfriends, including a Labradoodle named Barley,
twice his size. Despite being bitten by little dogs Alvin has never
once retaliated. He is truly an ambassador for his breed.'*

Amber is a 12-year-old girl who recently arrived at Dogs Trust Shoreham branch (01273 452 576) after her owner was taken into care. She is shy and wary of strangers in case they hurt her, so she would need time to build up trust, and an adult-only home with no other dogs. Her back legs are stiff so she can't walk that far, but you would need to be able to throw her tennis ball for her to fetch. She dreams of having her own garden to potter around in.

Amber
The Collie Cross

I dream of the high Welsh hills
And the sheep scattered and scurrying
And I am worrying at their heels
Rounding them, driving them
Hurrying into the pen.

I dream that my limbs are young again
And I'm running as fast as the gull flies
For the fox with the sun in his eyes
Who has not seen me.

I dream of the owner I had
And the sad day we parted
When I was brought here broken-hearted
Scared and suspicious
Bidding dreams goodbye.

I know there may never be
A second chance for me
Though I am gentle with the trusted
Grateful for the days I've had
Glad of the days to come
And yet I dream of a home.

Amber

The Greyhound

Squeezing her little almond eyes
Amber the Dog from Paradise
Is trying hard to interpose
Her dainty feet and pointy nose.
She lets out little high-pitched sounds
When cuddles are given to other hounds.
She wants them all, or gets distraught.

She 'came from Heaven', or so she thought:
Her owner 'worshipped her' more or less
And treated her 'in the nicest way'
And nobody now can bear to say
Amber, he let you go, princess.
Her owner was 'kind and loved her so'.
Amber my dear, he let you go.

*Born in 1996, Amber is one of the youngest and most recent
additions to Cindy and Tony Hilling's Essex household from the
Retired Greyhound Trust. Says Cindy: 'Amber is a singing
greyhound who loves the sound of her own voice. She demands your
attention.' The pretty brindle sings at certain television programmes
and whines during what she considers unnecessary conversations
between humans.*

Angell (the double 'l' in his name was 'to make him sound more masculine') came to Cindy and Tony Hilling from Seesaw Animal Sanctuary at two years old. His was born on 11th September 2003 – the Hilling Hounds actually have their birthdays celebrated. His owner had wanted to have him put to sleep. The Hillings were alerted to his plight by their niece, a veterinary nurse, and the kind people at Seesaw Sanctuary picked Angell up and brought him to what greyhound rescue people call his 'forever' home.

Angell

My owner had me put to sleep
When I was only two.
Before the vet could clinch the crime
I woke up in the nick of time
And pell-mell – off I flew.

You get two types of angell dogs:
There's 'outdoor' and 'indoor'
And as my tail is rather small
I don't fly verticall at all –
I fly round on the floor.

When dogs are indoor angels just
Their wings are made of light
But when you look up in the sky
Whole outdoor ones go sailing by
Invisiball to sight.

Barney, now 13, was given a home six years ago by Mary and Gary Martin after his owner, Gary's dad, emigrated to Spain. Mary: 'We were pleased to take him on,' though Barney had certain naughty ways. He would slyly sleep on their bed while they were out and if they came home early 'he would come down the stairs grumbling and growling.' He knocks the phone off the hook if it rings and will not tolerate the theme tunes of TV soaps - he starts barking. 'He wants non-stop stroking and will nudge you if you tire.'

Barney

A steady dog am I:
Not in a flurry.
I never fight or fly
Or whine or worry.
I see a lot of other dogs
Get in a lather
Barking and brawling in the sun.
That's why I'd rather
Be just a steady dog.

A steady dog am I:
What's past is perished.
I don't look back and cry
For what I cherished.
I see a lot of rescue dogs
Sorrowing over those they knew
But I'm just glad I'm here with you
To be your steady dog.

Bess

I was called Bolts and my sister was Nails.
Bad naughty Bolts! they said, bad naughty Nails!
We'd go hell for leather, rip roaring together
and flinging ourselves in a flailing fierce
Furfight flat out for cats' tails.
Off to the RSPCA with you, those owners said.
Somebody took us though, somebody brave...
Skirmishes over looks, scrummages over smells
We'd still knock seven bells
out of each other and couldn't behave.
Back to the RSPCA. So I said to Nails
It's your blasted fault – now we're banged up all day.
But Nails could do languid looks. Poor little soul they said
Petting and patting her head like a pup.
So Nails gets picked up! Well, I stood and stared.
Never a bark was heard. Never a tear was shed.
What about me? I said – nobody cared. So then I got scared.
Good job this couple came tossing a ball.
Now that's what I call
A top game for dogs of ability, dogs of agility
Dogs of nobility like me to play. I was in thrall!
Suddenly I had a hearth and a home
And a seaside to roam and two cuddlers to lick,
Woods and long walkies and games with a stick.
They don't say 'naughty Bolts'. Now I'm 'sweet Bess'.
What a good time I get now I'm these people's pet:
Living the high life – that's girl power I guess.

Bess's owners are Penny and John Avant. They spotted her on New Year's Day, 2007 at Exeter RSPCA, where she had given up barking and was about to give up altogether. They brought her home and she was eager to learn 'so long as treats were involved'. Says Penny: 'We were told she was between four and five years old. Bess is a wonderful companion, smiling first thing in the morning and sitting on our feet whenever possible.' Her new hobbies are running in circles (to acclaim), playing fetch and leaping waves on the beach.

Born in April 1996, Billy ended up at Danaher RSPCA, Wethersfield. Bev Farrell: 'He was just sitting there quietly, looking up with big brown eyes and a sweet sad face.' When they got him home 'he was a nightmare, and nipped my sons as they tried to stop him scavanging in dustbin bags.' Weeks of hell later, Billy was about to go back to the RSPCA. 'But my youngest son was mortified and pleaded with us to give him one more chance. Now Billy is the sweetest dog you could ever meet and very popular in the village. He helps my partner Steve when he's preparing the cricket pitch, loves to attend the matches and really looks forward to the cricket tea.'

Billy

I'm Billy the Cricket from Wickham St Paul:
Bum on the boundary, eye on the ball.
I expect any day to be summoned to Lord's as
My efforts at cricket have won me awards.
They've twice made me Clubman (and Dog) of the Year
(bit like Man of the Match but you don't get the beer).
Admittedly I've never played in a Test
But they don't make you Mascot unless you've impressed!
It's difficult when you've a talent like mine
To hold back your paw so that others may shine.
I've sat there and stewed when they've fumbled a catch
And I've seethed while some nincompoop lost us the match,
And of course all the worry has taken its toll:
Just look at my face, which was once black as coal.
I suffer in silence, but must draw the line
When I see on a Green that is rightfully mine
Big oafs playing football, it grieves me to say,
And my wickets and pitches mucked up in this way.
Which is why I rush in to prevent such foul play.
That's not cricket! I yell, as I dribble the ball.
Not footie! Not here! Not in Wickham St Paul!

Bonnie

The Maltese Dog

When I am dark she doth all brightness make
Her jewel eyes outwitting my great cares
Beckoning me with quivers and with stares
To join her in her world and in her wake.
Business she shows me, precious truth and sense
(Urgent she moves for time is short as limbs):
Leaves she must toss and earth with wonders brims
That she must scent and snuff with needs intense.
Careless of self, this little stranger came
To guard me, fierce and faithful, while I sleep
Giving her fragile strength, her passions deep
A mighty being in a tiny frame.
Who dares call her a cast-off and a toy
Knows not such vibrant and redeeming joy.

Little Bonnie is the guardian of author and Daily Mail *advice columnist Bel Mooney. Bonnie was found abandoned, tied to a tree in Bath. She is tiny but fearless and, as explained in Bel's moving autobiographical* Small Dogs Can Save Your Life, *helped her owner survive the break-up of her first marriage. Bonnie resembles the faithful lapdog of Mary Queen of Scots, found under her skirts after her beheading at Fotheringhay Castle, and this is why the sonnet form seemed right for her.*

Bonnie
The Greyhound

A nervy dog, feeling her way
When others bowed their heads and put a spurt on,
Bonnie the backmarker, shy and scared
Wasn't the sort of hound you hung your shirt on.
Shrinking in shadows, fated to be a loser
Bonnie backed off. She baulked. No one would choose her.

But then the big day dawned, and the Great Frost.
The air was tense, the starters on their toes.
And there it stood: their outside water bowl
Glittering hard with ice.
The dogs' blood froze.
Oh who would dare to test it? What brave nose?

Worried and wary, leaders all fell back.
It looked as though no dog would quench its thirst.
When suddenly, bowing her head with fiery eyes
from nowhere through the pack black Bonnie burst.
Champion Bonnie laid hold of the prize
And seized the ice between her jaws
And shook it till the spangles flew about
And scattered the pieces with her paws.
Lumps of light. Bits of sun.

And Bonnie danced. Bonnie had won.

Clarks Farm, at Little Totham near Maldon in Essex, is one of the most successful branches of the Retired Greyhound Trust, having re-homed hundreds of ex-racers. Bonnie was one of them. She was born on November 20th, 2005 and went to join Cindy and Tony Hilling's large greyhound family. They named her because of her coy, pretty face. She is a shy dog but 'very loving and caring'. Her poem describes a strange little incident that Cindy related to me.

Bracken is one of the thirteen Hilling Hounds of Essex and their only Lurcher. He was born in 2006 and has lived on the edge ever since, racing round the paddock obstacle course, diving through the cloth sausage, hurling himself after balls and grabbing visitors by the shoulders for a quick waltz. The Hillings describe him as 'a real live wire who likes to be the life and soul of the party. Always up to mischief and a very happy dog who loves his family.' It is unlikely that he will ever tire.

Bracken

I'm Bracken, I'm barmy.
They all try to calm me.
I'm bonkers, I'm up in your face.
I'm a climber, a jumper,
A bouncer, a bumper
With one ear all over the place.

I'm a Lurcher, a barger,
A writher, a charger,
I'm not like these greyhounds you see.
I'm a bounder, I'm bolder,
One leg on your shoulder –
Oh don't look at them – look at me!

They took me for training
But I'd be there straining:
I like to live life to the max!
I know why they dump us –
For riot and rumpus.
I'm Bracken, and these are the facts.

Bran

When I got out of jail I was well hard -
They wouldn't make a nice boy out of me.

From day one I wreaked havoc on their home.
Their shiny cooker? Covered it in wee.
I wrecked their sofa, stole their things.
A war of wills they'd have to face.
I'd win. I'd drive them to despair.
I'd show these humans. Wicked race.
And every day they'd comfort me
Saying 'dear Bran, it's all OK'
And every day I'd pay them back:
Destroy, defy and disobey.

But gradually love took its toll
I felt it working on my will
And something pulling on my soul
A clasp, a cuddle strong as steel.

So yes, they won. And yes, I drew.
And now I serve them all I can.
I'd lost my head. Another grew –
 A nice boy by the name of Bran.

Bran's owner Michelle Hailey found him nine years ago at Margaret Aldridge's very happy and well-run little shelter in White Colne, Essex. But being dumped at six months for not resembling a whippet had given Bran attitude, and phobias about thunder, bang noises, kittens, cows, cameras and statues of animals. A 'tornado' indoors, he also 'pulled up plants, dug holes and ate his dog leads and collars. He left presents of poo on the floor, usually containing a free plastic toy that he had devoured.' Castration and a Lurcher pal, Celt, saved the day. Says Michelle: 'He has made our lives very happy and we couldn't wish for better dogs.'

Brandy came from the Danaher Rescue Centre at Wethersfield in Essex, which is independent but affiliated to the RSPCA. Diana Hulkes was looking for another dog after the loss of her beloved Willow (see Willow the Shepherd Cross) as 'that had left a big hole both for me and my Labrador Bess'. Diana ended up choosing something completely different from what she intended. It was meant to be! 'Four years old when I had her, Brandy is six now, and you couldn't wish for a better companion.'

Brandy

Happened to have a shelter handy:
Got any German Shepherd girls?
Any age, but calm and waggy.
Oh – short-coated – some are shaggy.
What did I come away with?
Brandy. Brandy was young.
Highly hairy. Highly strung.
Home two hours, she wanted walkies.
Desperate – you can't resist.
Dragged me down three flights of steps.
Hit the concrete. Broke my wrist.
And then there was the training.
That was tough. I made a list.
No one to make sudden moves.
No one to raise their voice or call.
No one to look her in the eye.
No one to look at her AT ALL.
Best not to make waves: don't sigh.
Keep her calm and keep her cool.
Plus she does not like the pool.
Well, people – and dogs – learn.
Two years on and you should meet her.
Who is this carefree, friendly creature?
Brandy high dives off the board:
Tom Daley's cousie.
True, the entry's not quite there
But then Tom doesn't have to wear
A furry cozzie does he.

Bryony

There in her pen she sat. Fat. Matted fur.
She'd been kept in a garage. She was four.
I almost couldn't meet her gaze.
A wave of shame for humankind.
For broken trust. For wretched days.
This was the second time I'd come
To look at dogs without a home.
We'd just lost our beloved friend:
The shock still fresh in my heart.
We still weren't sure.

'Take her for a walk' I heard.
I jollied her past the pens
And trotted her past her past
Thinking this won't go far;
But as I turned to take her back
She struck out for our car.
Opened the door and she embarked.
Oh thank *you – you arrived at last.*
And so it was that Bryony came home
So strangely home: so strongly felt
That somehow she'd been here before.
Made friends with Paddy our Labrador:
The two of them lay back to back
Slumbering soundly on the floor.
And oh the pampering she now had!
The sweet shampoos, the walks to slim
The special foods, the cosseting
For such a lady, and for sure
She did deserve it all, and more.
So grateful, peaceful with her past
So happy to be home at last
No longer wary of our garage door.

On a visit to Danaher Rescue Centre in Wethersfield, Essex, Jon Hunt
chose Bryony, or rather she chose him. 'She came for a weekend trial
visit and stayed with us for just over eleven years. She was gentle,
loving and loyal, and she adored our old Labrador Paddy. Bryony was
a great help in the house – pulling sheets off the bed and tearing up
newspapers for the fire. She was a sock-stealer as well as a heart-
stealer. We feel she still walks with us along her secret paths in the
woods.'

Donna

Donna, dog. Escape artiste.
Cat burglary considered.
Can manage mortise locks with teeth
But bolts are better *sliddered*.

No job too small, like oven door,
Fridge freezer, bag or bin.
No gate so great I can't get out
Or hatch I can't get in.

I'm black, elusive, quiet and neat
And won't grass out a chum.
Donna.com. Apply on line
But watch your bloomin' bum .

*Apart from being adept at breaking and entering, Donna is secretly
'very quiet and a born worrier,' according to owners Cindy and Tony
Hilling. She enjoys her walks and feels safe in the field and paddock
near her home, but on the whole prefers to stay indoors. She is terrified
of thunderstorms and 'generally finds the world a scary place.' She
came from Romford Greyhound Owners' Association. Donna was
born in 1999 and celebrates her birthday on 30th August.*

Dudley

A dog of literary mind
Deserves the best:
Fine books, fine sandwiches I find
Dotted around the desks
Of Watson Little Limited -
The agents I employ
To scour the globe for meaty tomes
They think I might enjoy.

An oeuvre (or some hors d'oeuvres) set in
An eatery in Cheam;
Some good chicklit, so long as it
Has chicken as its theme;
A narrative that grabs my nose
And tastebuds right away
Concerning tuna mayonnaise
And death in some café.
Originality is key:
For me the sure-fire winner
Has well-drawn characters
Extolling what they had for dinner.

This firm is good, though I will say
They are a touch familiar
Calling me 'Doodlebug', 'Del Boy'
And some things even sillier.
They need to bear in mind that I
Am not just some mere writer.
I'm Dudley Little - gastronome
And all-round clever blighter.

Dudley belongs to Mandy Little, managing director of literary agents Watson Little in London. While not exactly on the staff, he is on the website, so feels entitled to spend his days 'scavenging and squeezing plastic squeaky toys' while people are trying to work. He came from Sutton Coldfield at the age of four via a website called PreLoved, and settled in very quickly. Dudley lists his hobbies as 'innovative fiction and pinching tuna sandwiches'.

Emma

She practised being a person
All her days. Studying me
Finding out how to do it.
I laughed at her little traits
But she was a person
And she knew it.
Followed my feet, my fate
Running beside my horse
Swaying her shoulders
Cornering in the car
Knowing to indicate (of course)

And where the best walks are...
Playing at hide and seek
Ready with infinite licks.
Lying across my lap
Having run out of tricks.

She never had a star.
She fixed on me
Her windblown person
Bringing up the rear
Following not from fear
But sheer delight.
Call her a dog if you like:
Nothing can quite erase
The light in her eager eyes
The oneness in all her ways.
These are the bonds that bind
Human and bird and beast.
No one was first or last.
Nothing that loves is least.

Emma, or 'Splod', a Beardie cross, was the beloved friend of Annie Christie from Gosfield in Essex. 'I rescued Emma in 1993 – the family had no control over her. She became my little "right hand man" and everywhere I went Emma was sure to follow. She loved long walks alongside my mare Ria, and being in the car, staring avidly at the indicator level as if to say "Go on then – indicate – I know where we're going!" I love all my other doggies, but there will never be another Emma. We were soul mates. I still miss her terribly.'

Eva

Brave little Eva, runt of the litter,
Straining her sinews, never a quitter,
Half their size but determined to beat them,
Taking two strides to their one to defeat them,
Eva the stayer, just as he'd trained her,
Working her muscles till everything pained her,
Master would love her for sure if she won
But dogs thundered past her.
Eva was done.

How could he leave her? How could he hurt her?
How could he throw her away and desert her?
Big as her heart was, sweet and unguarded,
Eva like thousands of others discarded,
Dumped in a meadow or shot in the head,
Buried in landfills, rubbished and dead.

Eva the graceful, Eva the charmer.
Nothing to strain her, nothing to harm her.
Cuddles for Eva, carefully tended,
Treasured and loved now that racing has ended.
Everything splendid.

But greyhounds have wrongs that can never be mended.

Another of the Hilling Hounds, Eva is a small, muscly girl with a funny run and black, glossy coat. I hear that black greyhounds are known in certain racing circles as 'dustbin bags' because there are so many of them and they are easily disposed of. Eva is extremely beautiful. She is cuddly with humans but enjoys trying to boss the rest of the household's dogs about, notwithstanding Alpha female Kesha. Eva came from the Retired Greyhound Trust and was born on 11th May 2004.

Herbert

I'm not having that.
Their blasted cockerel fluttering at me.
So I snarl up a storm.
That shuts him up. That fixes him, all right.
No, I'm not having that.
I'm not having crows, rooks, riffraff
On my land. Or rats rooting about.
I snuffle them all out.
One snap and it's good night.
Gone with one bite, as I'm not having that.
Shepherd Dog Bonzo?

He's allowed to live
Here in my house. I warn him now and then
By latching on his ear.
He's never piped up once.
No fear. He knows just what he'd get
As I'm not having that.
Dogs in the street I've met?
I look them in the eye.
'Want a trip to the vet?' I say.
And then I just let fly, as I'm not having that.
They got me out of Battersea
Especially to run this farm.
Sharing that tractor with my Dad.
Yes, I worked hard - I did my part.
That's why I'm boss. And yet I've got a heart.
Not an unfeeling chap, no. Not a cad.
When we lost my Mum's olden dog
Missus got very sad.
I said as I jumped on her lap:
'Don't worry Mum - You've still got me.
You see? It's not all bad.'

Annie Christie of Gosfield in Essex, Herbert's owner: 'His name is very apt. He is a feisty little boy, but he was very sweet and supportive when I lost my dear dog Emma. Herbie came to us very hand-shy. If you put your hand out to stroke him he would snap at your fingers. You must watch him with other dogs because he gets himself in fight mode. He loves Bonzo and cuddles up to him, but he will occasionally latch on to Bonzo's ear, in case he wants a fight. Poor Bonzo doesn't – he is very subservient - but Bert is just checking.'

Jasmine

All the orphans, all the needy
All the battered and the broken
All the lost ones of Nuneaton
All are nuzzled on arrival:
All are welcomed at the shelter
Washed with lickings, washed with kisses
Washed and welcomed there by Jasmine
Patron Saint of the Unwanted.
Tiny pups, a pair of foundlings,

Tied on railway lines to die
Lifted by the scruff with whining
Placed so softly on the sofa
Jasmine settling, Jasmine nestling
Fox cubs, badger cubs and chickens
Nursing guinea pigs and rabbits
Letting birds perch on her long nose
(Jasmine could not hurt a fly).
Bramble, little roe deer baby
Found half-conscious in a meadow
Weak and wobbly, Jasmine mothered
Cuddling, covering with kindness
Trotting with him round the kennels
Eight legs mingling in their motion.
Did she learn to be so tender
From the sweetness of her owners?
No. We found her frightened, frail
Locked up and abused, abandoned.
Never judge books by their covers
Nor a dear dog by its tale.

*In 2003 police in Warwickshire broke into an abandoned garden shed
and discovered a very frightened, starving female greyhound. She had
obviously been abused. They took her to Nuneaton Warwickshire
Wildllife Sanctuary (0247 634 5243), where she joined all the other
lost and abandoned animals rescued by Geoff Grewcock and his team.
'Jasmine', as they called her, somehow felt she had been appointed to
help run the place and welcome new waifs. She set about licking and
mothering fox cubs, rabbits, pups, badger cubs, birds, chicks, guinea pigs
and an 11-week-old roe deer fawn. Years later beautiful Jasmine is still
there, helping Geoff rescue the unwanted.*

Jo

A fine tenth birthday I'd get: You'd think they'd have a care.
You're not ten very often, and even then it's rare.
They'd take me somewhere surely where dogs can romp and roam:
A seashore or a meadow, a disused aerodrome.
No – Glastonbury Abbey. What larks I should have there.
A fossil with no meat on, a dark and dogless prayer.
We waddled to our picnic: 'ALL DOGS ON LEADS' it said.
This called for concentration: a sharp jerk of my head
Then collar off and bingo! Around that place I tore:
Legs going like the clappers, lungs billowing for more.
I did a princely circuit, a round-the-ruins race.
I felt I'd done a good job, and livened up the place.
They think I'm not religious, but who could truly say
The spirit wasn't on me, when I was ten that day?

*The author's big blue ex-racer Jo came from the Clarks Farm branch of
the Retired Greyhound Trust at Little Totham in Essex, where staff have
actually re-homed a thousand other cast-off racers. Jo had eight wins at
Catford before he was lamed and discarded. To the shelter staff he was
known as 'G.O.G.' (Grumpy Old Git) for nipping dog bottoms or tails
that poked through his cage. But he was recuperating from a broken leg
and besides, he was very aristocratic. Yes, the embarrassing incident
described actually happened, and Jo is pictured just after his
accomplishment.*

Jody

I'm Jody and I'm beautiful
So elegant in my chair.
You'd think I were posing for *Country Life*
Or modelling doggie wear.

My eyes are my best feature
When I turn my head to the side
To set off my pretty profile –
Another source of pride.

My coat is of burnished copper
Enhancing my slender waist.
That they should have dumped such a beautiful girl
Just shows they had no taste.

One of the large Hilling family of rescue greyhounds, Jody, born 7th March 2001, came originally from the village of Gestingthorpe in Essex. Cindy Hilling explains: 'Her owner had died in his bungalow and when they were found Jody was sitting with him, waiting for him to wake up. Jody came to us at four years of age. She is a steady, easy girl to look after and very well behaved.' Jody is also very photogenic and knows it. She likes to sit in armchairs posing and fluttering her eyelashes.

Kesha

Kesha wasn't thought worth her keep.
They wanted her winning not half asleep.
They'd give her a kick or a poke with a stick
But she still wasn't keen and she still wasn't quick.

She wasn't a looker they might perhaps flog –
They thought she looked more like a rat than a dog.
Whoever would want her? Just look at that snout
With her chin sticky-in and her nose sticky-out.

So they got rid of Kesha, but everyone knows
That with rescue and love a girl blooms like a rose.
Her eyes lit with sparkles, her face filled with fun
And no one is keener than Kesha to run.

Before she was discarded for losing her edge, Kesha had had a very successful racing career. Says Cindy Hilling, who got her from the RGT: 'She didn't retire until aged five, which is late for a racing greyhound. Kesha loves people, adores children and is very much in charge of all our other greyhounds. She has welcomed many into our home over the years.' Despite her grey hairs (she was born on 2nd September 1996) Kesha is head of food bowls, seating and use of paddock.

Kim belonged to Jon and Anne Hunt in Gosfield, Essex. Says Jon: 'So many people let him down. He was anxious at first – ate a whole half a pound of butter! Love and loyalty grew. He became a good friend of our Labrador Paddy, and eventually they shared the Top Dog position. As an old boy, Kim suffered a severe stroke. We thought the end was near, but seeing us on what we thought was our final visit to the vet to say goodbye, he rallied and enjoyed another six months with us. We feel he is still here.'.

Kim

Kim looked yet again in their bowls.
Nothing. No food. No water. Mistress gone.
A carer who did not care –
And he had already lost one home,
Barking his anguish in the night:
Somebody come! Somebody come!
Nature made Mongrels stern
To bear often bitter blows,
To lead often loveless lives;
But hardness and harshness take their toll
Of even the brave with an empty bowl.
Just as skylarks and poets soar
High above a humble start
By listening hard and sensing far,
Mongrels too can raise the bar
Though all seems lost and all hope gone
Extending a nose towards a star.
So when the special visitor left
Kim made a final bid supreme
To break his bonds and hunt his dream
And he followed far in the tracks of the car
For miles and days through storm and hail,
With never a flag or a wag of his tail
Until at last Kim and the man
Were reunited in the rain
Never to be lost again.
And Kim went home and as was due
One humble Mongrel dream came true.

Lessa

In the presence of Lessa
You feel your nose twitch:
You prick up your ears and you sense far away
A fiend or a fire
(You're not yet sure which)
And you know that you will not be walking today.

In the presence of Lessa
The hair-raising men
Are coming with guns for herself and her litter,
To use her for hunting
To hurt her and hit her
And cage her, and leave the dog yearning and wanting.

In the presence of Lessa
You get the idea
That the green of our land in the glint of our sun
Is a blessing best felt
By a heart that's known fear
And you relish your moments, with her, one by one.

Our Lessa is cherished.
Our Lessa is safe.
Our Lessa's no longer a Cypriot waif
With a hell for a home where so many have perished.
We wish we could tell her that all is secure
But she twitches her nose, as she's never quite sure.

Lessa lives with her owners Keith and Margaret Miller and gorgeous rough collie Lass in the village of Ravenstone, Buckinghamshire. She came to England from Cyprus with Keith and Margaret after they successfully founded a huge modern dog rescue centre on the island, battling with politicians and bureaucrats and saving the lives of hundreds of dogs from cruelty and neglect. Lass and Daisy (another rough collie, who survived distemper) came over to join the Millers' English dogs Hestia, Aurora and Bacchus.

Mabel

Lord Byron was a proud man: strong and proud.
But Byron would have wept to see her chained
Her jowls drooping, eyes trained on the ground.
Boswain, his Newfoundland and one true friend
Had looked so like her, this great bear of a dog:
Mighty and gentle, faithful to the end.
But that was worshipped. This was just despised.
Mabel – a picture of neglect
Her thick coat knotted and matted
As she shuffled the length of her chain
And seeing no hope at the end of it
Shuffled back again.
In three years she'd been let off only twice.
She ran away. They got her back again.
But why? Why ever did they buy
A beast to be a burden and a dread?
Whatever status could she give
When all she wanted was to live
With those she loved, who might love her?
Those she could watch, and guard with fealty
And maybe a child or two to stroke her head
and hug her tight – as they do now
Burying their faces in her fur.
Perhaps Lord Byron brought us to that sight
To save her, bring her home and treat her right.

Mabel was rescued by Carol Anderson and Tracey Doyle of Pattiswick in Essex in September 2009. 'She was roughly two-and-a-half. She had already had two other homes and spent all her time chained.' Initially because of muscle wastage she was 'unable to walk round our garden, let alone further afield.' Now she can do a two-mile hike, has a regular cut and blow dry and loads of cuddles. 'She adores children, in particular our son Thomas, of whom she is very protective.' Despite trips to beaches and rivers, this Newfoundland 'refuses to get her feet wet – you try shifting 55 kgs.'

Millie

Bouncing is good. I love to bounce.
And flounce and dance and twirl. I'm lithe.
An energetic girl. I'm light as air.
I'd float up if it were not for my hair.
My mistress calls me Milliedog. Or Millie Moo.
Or was it Millipede? Not sure. I'll check.
No, just the four. My lively legs that carry me away
Away away from rackets and alarm.
The mowers, hoovers and the drills.
That screen for giving humans thrills -
That blares out. That could do me harm.

I once got out and shot off to the wood
And got benighted. Lost my way.
My fringe, you see. Unsighted. Yes I
Did get back OK. But they were frantic.
They thought I'd hitchhiked
Round to Harwich bound for the Atlantic.
I lose things, yes. Like balls. They just go missing.
My pups all disappeared. That's right.
One minute I was kissing them:
The next they'd gone – and litter after litter.
The more I had, the more they disappeared.
Made an exhaustive search.
Gone. Done a flitter. And what's really weird –
The humans gone to boot.
Cleared off to Spain. Good riddance to bad eggs.
They'd sold my babes for gain and banked the loot.
Good job I have a proper owner now –
Those others can't compete.
Thank goodness for my mad and lively legs.
'She tumbled but she landed on her feet.'

*Millie the Bearded Collie was adopted by Emma's owner Annie
Christie from a rescue centre in Lincolnshire in March 2008. She
and her brother had been used for breeding and then discarded, the
owners having decamped to Spain. 'Millie is typical of the breed –
slightly neurotic. She gets scared of the sound of drills, hoovers and
mowers and will run and hide. Our other dogs all love a game of
ball, but Millie finds it hard to locate a ball because of her fringe.'*

Oliver

Ollie is flowing in the wind.
His ears, as he sits in the car,
Ripple gently like the hair
Of an actress in an old film noire.
Ollie has lost some teeth.
His grin is a little sucked in,
The hairy chin beneath.

Ollie adores his Mum
Such that, when she comes home,
He throws back his head and howls:
Howls from his deepest tum.

Except when she returned
From the Hip Op.
Would not greet.
Would not speak.
Sat with his back to her for a week.

Ollie the obstinate boy
Cannot be bustled when late.
If he wants to sit, he'll sit.
If he wants to go back, that's it.

Oliver, proud as a prince.
Third home lucky, happy ever since
(Apart from the business of the Op
Which did necessitate a strop).

Oliver was born in Cyprus, and was rescued from his miserable existence by an Englishwoman and brought back to Britain. Sadly the lady fell ill and died and her family decided to move to America, so poor Ollie was homeless once again. That was until he met Mrs Audrey Crawley of Halstead in Essex – it was love at first sight. Daughter Marian finds Ollie can sometimes be 'a monkey' about going for walkies or getting in the car, but Audrey couldn't wish for better: 'He is an excellent, loyal and brilliant housedog and companion.'

Otto the Lurcher started life as 'Munchie'. He and his sister Pickles were stolen as puppies from Dogs Trust Evesham Rehoming Centre in October 2009. Five months on and 171 miles away in Kent, a lone emaciated pup was found running round a hospital car park. Identified from his microchip, Munchie was taken to Dogs Trust Canterbury where he caught the eye of Tessa and Stuart Wheeler, owners of Chilham Castle. Says Tessa: 'I found myself instantly taken by Munchie.' Now known as 'Otto', he presides over 320 acres and hopes soon to be 'mingling' on their garden open days.

Otto

Stolen in the dead of night:
Caught with Pickles by the scruff.
Shoved in cages out of sight
And driven off.
Rough men speeding us away
Taking us we knew not where.
Pickles nuzzles me to say
'Evesham's back there!'
Bundled out in some strange land.
Waited till their guard was down.
Wrestled from a filthy hand
And ran to town.
'Someone help me – I've come far!
I'm a pup, and desperate!'
Warden took me in his car
And to the vet.
Rubbed me with a Meter Peeper.
Found the chip that said my name.
Called the Dogs' Trust as my keeper.
Dogs' Trust came!
Happy ending to my story.
Lady saw me hang my head
Missing little Pickles sorely.
'You shall live in style,' she said.
Now I am her castle keeper,
Grounds as far as I can spy.
All this from a chip and Peeper.
(This is not a porkie pie.)

Ouzo

The Dogs of Greece live to be three
If they are lucky and can flee
The bullets and the poisoned snacks
The wheels, the waiters and the whacks.

Careering under carts and cars
They haunt the restaurants and bars
Skinny and scared round tourists' feet
Begging for mercy and for meat.

Amid this hell a darling girl
Became our little sentinel:
Covered in ticks, a lively soul
She seemed to have a dream, a goal.
She'd entertain, charm and amuse
And make off with your clothes or shoes.

But when we left, we saw her grieve
Dogging us in a desperate state.
How could a faithful heart conceive
That we would leave her to her fate?

We begged and bribed for her release.
Nine months of worry, work and wait
Got her to Gatwick in a crate.
She's here! Goodbye, mean streets of Greece.

Rob and Helen Simpson were on holiday on the Greek island of Zakynthos when they spotted Ouzo roaming the streets. She would beg for sausages and chicken. Says Helen Simpson: 'When we got home we went on the internet and discovered Zakynthos Dog Rescue. Two very kind English ex-pat ladies helped us get Ouzo rounded up. Sadly when they got her into the van her doggie friend tried to follow, but they couldn't take him.' Ouzo now lives in Long Melford, Suffolk. When she smells sausages and chicken cooking she jumps for joy.

Penny came from Romford Greyhound Owners and is one of the Hilling troupe of rescue greyhounds on the borders of Essex and Suffolk. She invariably looks worried, as she has a lot of parenting problems. Cindy Hilling: 'She is a real mum to her dozens of furry toys and is usually to be found with one of her "babies" in her mouth. She once woke us up at three in the morning in order to rescue a baby she had left outside.' Penny was born in 2001 and her birthday is 5th September.

Penny

Penny finds babies everywhere:
Anything furry, soft or round
She carefully carries to her bed
And nestles down.
She piled eleven teddies in a mound
And sat there waiting to hatch her brood.
They did not stir - they were very good.

Penny was slightly troubled though.
She thought one or two might
have whimpered at least, but no.

Turning them over with her nose
She wondered had she done wrong?
Other mothers had wriggly ones
That made a mess and made a pong
But Penny's just seemed to doze.
Ah well, she thought, I'm a wonderful mum.
I expect my wriggly ones will come.

Labrador Ray, who looks as though he might have seen the very vision described in his poem, was handed over to Dogs Trust by a family from Essex in March 2008. They'd had him from a pup but sadly gave him up because they felt they couldn't cope with him any more in their busy household. He was very well trained and loved walks, swimming, retrieving and rewards. Thank goodness Ray was re-homed locally in August 2009.

Apologies to William Wordsworth, but Ray (Dogs Trust West London branch) needed a home

Ray

I wandered lonely as a Peke
That preens and prances out of doors
When all at once I saw a clique
A host of Golden Labradors
Beside the lake, beneath the trees
Cocking their legs upon the breeze.

As ravenous as dogs that dine
Yet hanker after Milky Way
They craned their necks and gave a whine:
Search him for grub! they seemed to say.
Ten thousand saw I at a glance
All eyeing me somewhat askance.

The thought occurred that I should run
Though I was mesmerised indeed
To see such splendour in the sun
And spy so many of my breed:
Yet one idea was uppermost:
Leg it you fool before you're toast.

Now oft when on my bed I lie
Relaxed and chilled in pensive mood
They flash upon my inward eye
When I am thinking of my food
And then my heart with pleasure soars
And dances with the Labradors.

Roseanna, born 20th October 2003, is another of the Retired Greyhound Trust ex-racers who share the home of Cindy and Tony Hilling, though she is their only 'blue'. Rosie is small and pretty but extremely alert. Her keen eyes are able to spot movement in a distant field and in the excitement her canines can sometimes be seen sticking out like small fangs. Cindy Hilling: 'Roseanna is soft and cuddly and good on the lead. Her favourite pastime is sunbathing on the grass.'

Roseanna

Roseanna, Roseanna, eyes on stilts
Seeing the cat on the fence.
The hare on the horizon
Makes her tense.

Roseanna, Roseanna, off the lead
Swift as the wind, sharp as a dart
Hunts until she hurts herself
And breaks her heart.

Roseanna, Roseanna, slow down, girl -
No need to go quite so fast.
But her little legs can't stop running
From the past.

Roxy and Jade

Shall I compare thee to a hirsute breed?
Thou art small streakers, sleek, without a tress.
Poor Pulis shake their manes, dreadlocked indeed
And Lhasas hate their hair but can't undress.
Sometimes too hot the Newfoundland's mop grows
And with a hose and bucket must cool down
And every Sheepdog double-coated goes
Unless by Flymo accidentally mown.
But thy black bodies shall be cool and free
Nor shall thy heads attract those fairies naughty
That may adhere to hairier hounds than thee
And make them itch, though they be high and haughty.
So long as dogs be mutts or best in show
So Jade and Roxy boldly bare may go.

Apologies to William Shakespeare but Jade and
Roxy (Dogs Trust Bridgend branch) needed a home

Seven-year-old Roxy and Jade, aged 10, ended up with Dogs Trust in April 2009 after the couple who owned them got divorced and the dogs were being left alone all day. According to branch staff they were wonderful dogs and quite inseparable but Roxy, when she arrived, was suffering from chronic dermatitis on all four feet. 'The condition improved dramatically in our care. They were re-homed together on 27th June last year.'

Sally, a Battersea girl, belonged to Betty Coppin of Gosfield in Essex, though she was originally spotted at the Dogs' Home by Betty's younger son. She was about six months old, and scared of her own shadow: 'She was thin and very nervous and would not go out at all.' However, Sally took to obedience like a duck to water and won many competitions – on her own terms. 'She had a mischievous streak in her,' says Betty. 'She would not do as bid until she got in the ring and then she would shine.'

Sally

Fearing freedom Sally shook
Feeling the shock of the new.
Battersea was all indoors.
Now on the hot train here she panted hard.
What was this world she had never seen?
What did it mean? she thought, wild-eyed.
Our house seemed safe, but not that door.
The front door opened its jaw:
She froze with fright.
Bony, her tummy tight, she watched me
Warily on a long lead, gardening
Showing her all was well.
Seemed safe enough – but not that brush!
Brushes would scare her all her life.
Slowly she grew more sure.
Jenny, a dog pal, helped her heal.
The shy dog now explored.
Classes – now this was more
The sort of thing she liked!
She found her paws. She loved the ring.
Wouldn't obey till she was in
But then she won, and shone.
I slept downstairs in the end
Beside my old friend, beautiful and bright.
So what if she couldn't make the stairs?
She'd made the stars all right.

Sam

With plods deliberate, feet slightly splayed,
Sam shuffles out to meet his guests.
His large brown clouded eyes survey the room.
'Why have they come?'
Because Sam found a home.
Because white whisker days are precious ones.

Keen not to do wrong
For six months Sam kept shtum.
We guessed the dog was dumb.
He'd been demoralised: no sound would come.
But as he waited for his food
A lust for life stirred in Sam's grizzled brow
And suddenly one stentorian note
Echoed from where he stood.
What's more, feeling the tingle in his throat,
Sam barked again, seeming quite proud.
He'd never thought it was allowed.

Rejected and dejected and forlorn
A broken down old boy, his dog dreams done,
Has wandered into joy.
Still mystified by where his woes have gone
Sam stares at his admirers, feels reborn
And fans an ancient tail.
His wags say words (where words would only fail)
'My dog star must have shone.'

'How did we find Sam? We saw a sad photograph in the paper. A sad-looking old dog, and a very sad story told by the staff at the rescue centre at Martlesham Heath. But a happy ending when Sam came to live with us. We only had eleven months with this dear old chap but they were eleven joyous months, and his spirit still roams the cottage and the garden.' – Jon and Anne Hunt, Gosfield in Essex.

*Born on 21st April 2004, Samantha is one of the abused greyhounds
rescued by the RGT and subsequently given a home by the
greyhound-loving Hillings of Essex. Samantha, who came originally
from Lincolnshire, stole the author's heart the moment she met her.
Once you have made friends she craves affection and just hates it
when you leave. Says Cindy Hilling: 'She has settled down really
well but she is still anxious around people she doesn't know and she is
inclined to pull on the lead.'*

Samantha

Samantha comes close, with narrow eyes
Her long nose searching.
A black dog, nothing special in her guise;
A tiny flash of white the sole relief
Above her temples, large from all her thinking.

Samantha comes for your caress
Offering all the gifts she has:
Her stillness and her gentleness.
And only then you spot the scars
Pocking her coat, her legs, her tail
Where the man stubbed out his cigarettes
And your thoughts fail.

All the religions of the world
Tell humankind where love is found
Yet none of them mentions,
Waiting for your humanity,
This gentle hound.

Sidney

A problem dog is someone who
After you've terribly kindly come
To rescue him and take him home
Leaps through the window of your car
And runs back in the shelter door;
Then, setting off for somewhere remote
Stands up behind, forelegs in play
And grasping them round the driver's throat
Throttles you on the motorway.

A problem dog is one who chews
Whenever you go out, and drags
Your carpet up against the door
Dismembering his toys, your shoes
And, most dramatically of all,
The sofa seats, leaving the bags.
A problem dog is one who grows
Steadily safe when left alone –
You will be back, this is his home –
Who puts behind him former woes,
And wags and welcomes you instead,
So even those who thought him bad
Grudgingly praise and pat his head.
A problem dog is one who steals
Your heart at last when it's too late:
When he is precious, old and grey
And loudly you lament his fate.
Treasure your problem dog because
One day it's certain, he'll leave you
Bereft and scared as he once was
With nothing suitable to chew.

Sidney McGee was the beloved gentle pal of the author when she lived in London. But he had not been home a week before her mother was pleading for him to go back whence he came (Wood Green Animal Shelter, Heydon). Despite problems with destruction while he was settling in, Sid turned out to have an angelic temperament and became known to all as 'Doglet'. In old age he developed a plump sailor's roll. A small boy, noticing this waddle, observed: 'Look Dad – that dog's going side by side.'

Sparky

There's a dog in a kennel over there
Named Splash. Someone should train him
And make that little monster mind
Before I brain him.
He's one of those Jack Russell tykes:
Done as he liked – you know the story.
Terriers are terrors – they're all muck or glory.
Try to look big, behave like bombs –
They're hell, those.
All up and down and in and out
Like fiddlers' elbows.
I know what I would do with him
But staff here, they're too nice.
I'd give him Splash –
I'd flush him down the loo, that's my advice.

Splash

There's a dog in a kennel
      over there
Bang out of order.
He's one of those Jack
      Russells –
He's a mad marauder.
He says he's full of energy –
      his name is Sparky.
I said you'll never find a home
With that malarkey.
He's got no manners – shows us up
At Darlington Dogs' Trust.
He thinks he's being cheeky
But he's not – he's *boisteruss*.
I know what I would do with him
But staff here, they're too gentle.
I'd stick a fuse up his behind
And light it, as he's mental.

These little terrors are to be found (in separate kennels) at Dogs Trust Darlington branch. Sparky 'is a cracking dog but he can be a little boisterous at times. He would like an adult-only home and a calm, confident owner who will not be phased by cheeky terrier behaviour.' Splash 'is a little dog, but no one seems to have told him that. He is a great character but he has been used to getting his own way a lot. Training staff here will be happy to advise on settling him in.' (Call Claire on 01325 335 952).

Stan

Stan was a GSD, or used to be:
Once worth a bit. But now as found
Shuffling the streets of Bucks.
Stan could hardly stand.
Had toenails inches long and puppy pads
That never touched the ground.
Front feet turned out, back legs unsound.
Colitis. Coconut mat for a coat.
Softly he sniffed my hand.
It hurt to see him grab his food
And aiming backwards
throw it down his throat.
He had to have eight teeth removed
Yet Stan was clean and proud:
Would howl to go to the loo.
My daughter rang me. 'Mum' she said,
'I've bathed Stan.' You've bathed who?
He lived indoors and slept beside my bed
His faithful face waiting as I was ill.
Having other down-and-out dogs
We couldn't pay the bill
for his teeth, his feet, his ops.
An appeal in Phonebox Magazine
Brought in the funds and fans
For Stan, the people's friend.
A poor dog, now a dear dog
And valued in the end.

Jayne Stevenson and her husband from Olney, Bucks, rescue down-and-out dogs. Says Jayne: 'Stan was in a terrible state. He'd been found wandering in East Wick, Olney, and we had him registered with Milton Keynes police as a serious neglect case. Stan could hardly walk. I put my hand out by way of greeting and he sniffed my hand, and that was it. I said "He's coming with us". His vet bills cost hundreds of pounds, so I wrote an article in Phonebox and kind readers made donations, and sent bedding. Stan had lots of fans. He became very popular, plodding about the market with me. We had him less than a year before he died, but he did have that happiness.'

Storm, a three-year-old white Huskie, belongs to Jo and Gary Berry and drags them about the streets of Long Melford, Suffolk. They kept seeing her picture on the window of the RSPCA shop in Bury St Edmunds, but Jo had said, 'No more dogs' after they lost their last one. Finally they gave in and went to the RSPCA shelter near Newmarket to see her. The blue eyes did it. Storm was evidently one of three, but she wasn't wanted. Now she's not only wanted but plans to play for England.

Storm

I drag my people at breakneck speed
Along the road upon my lead.
They love it as they scream and flail
Trying to slow me to no avail.
I did some barking once or twice:
A trainer came to give advice.
I barked at her until she left.
I bark and bark until their deaf-ed.
I like to bark from my window seat
Or lie there trying to shock the street.
A neighbour hurried in to say
'Her naughty bits are on display!'
Huskies, they'll tell you, will never play.
But over our back fence one day
There came this beautiful, bouncy treat -
Boys make them go up with their feet.
They shouted: 'Throw it over, mate!'
But no, you have to confiscate.
It had a lot of roundness to it
But I found if you bite or chew it
It gives a hiss. Then it goes flat
And flollops – I was enthralled by that.
So now I shake it in my teeth
Or crawl round with it underneath:
It's pretty old and pretty slack
But NOBODY'S going to get it back.

Sugar

I'm big. They may put me in a bag
And dump me out at sea.
Those vets – they stick you with sharp spines.
They tried to poison me.
They gave me pills to shut me up –
I knew too much, could be.
The Council came and caught me
Running round Surrey Heath.
Oh look – there's one of them devil dogs
With the fifty rows of teeth.
Get the snare, mate! Get the lorry!
We'll sling a net on her, don't worry.

Yet I'm a sweet, sweet girl –
Ask anyone who knows me well.
I love a kiss and cuddle.
It's just that I'm in a muddle
With all these shocks and scary men –
I won't let them mess with me again
As I'm a sweet, sweet girl.
I want an owner firm and kind,
An owner who can change my mind
About the human breed.
I'm waiting here with baited breath
So I can lick them half to death.
Big love is what I need.

Sugar is waiting and hoping at Dogs Trust Harefield branch in West London (01895 453930), where she arrived as a stray from Surrey Heath Borough Council. Staff say Sugar is 'a sensitive girl who needs a quiet home and someone experienced with powerful breeds that will give her time to settle in. She's wary of new people, especially men, and dislikes formal handling and seeing vets. She would need help with socialisation, but once Sugar knows you she loves nothing more than cuddles.'

Tiger and Tilly

Waste not want not
Thought Tiger and Tilly, tucking in
To the bag of birdseed on the floor.
Their owner found them grainy-nosed
And asked them sternly who did what.
'That Tilly started it', thought Tiger
Which was an utter lie.
His ball-of-fire behaviour
Meant they couldn't go far
Or travel anywhere in the car
Due to his lathered barking
At passing dogs and passers-by.
It brought shame on them both,
Poor Tilly thought
For she was dainty in her ways.
But she was Tiger's pride and all his stars:

Tilly being from Venus

And Tiger being from Mars.

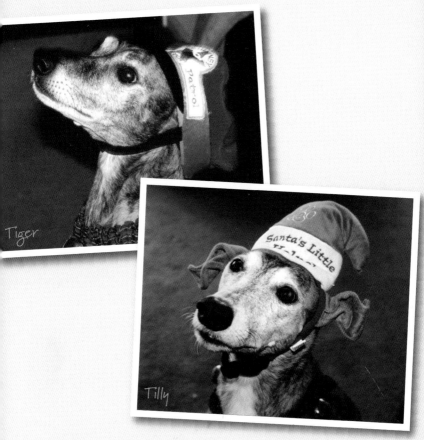

Tiger

Tilly

Tiger is 14 and Tilly is 12. They have lived with Claire Hannan for seven years since she spotted them at the RSPCA Wethersfield shelter in Essex. The two were about to be split up as nobody wanted the pair, but this would have broken their spirits. The lovers are inseparable. Tiger barks with fury at all comers if he is out with Tilly, and 'if you try to take Tiger out without Tilly she will hurl herself at the door to be with him'. They sleep together wrapped in Claire's duvet, play together and eat together, including the bag of seed.

Tim

The Labrador

Jack Frost hurt with his nips.
How he gnawed at my ear tips.
Not a fair fight. I couldn't bite
Him back – all my fight was numb.
I heard my so-called humans in the house
Laughing and playing with their other dogs
All dry and warm.
I was the runt they hardly fed
Shuddering and shivering
Out in a battered kennel for my bed.
I felt Jack's cold clench hard
Trying to have my heart
Trying to turn me blue.
But dogs are made of love and we stay true:
Even the coldest, even the most forlorn.
And I just knew
That Big Tall Man would come
And take me somewhere warm
And kind. That I would find
A family, a spaniel pal, a home.
I am a dog of love and I just knew.
Yet when it did come true
I couldn't hold my joy
And though I'm a clean boy
and never overflow
That once I weed in their hall
And let my feelings show.

Tim, who is now about two, was saved from a place in Suffolk by a volunteer with the Labrador Lifeline Trust, John Westgate. He is adored by his new Norfolk family and their Cocker Spaniel Winnie, from whom he is inseparable. He has made a complete recovery from his cold life and frostbitten ears. Says the charity's Anne Carter: 'Each day he seems to take another step forward. It is only through the love and kindness shown by his adopted family that this little dog now lives a normal and happy life.'

Timmy – very young, wiry, glossy and extremely scarred – is the most recent addition to the Hilling household in Essex. The first night he spent in his happy new home he slept not a wink in case it was all too good to be true. The second night tiredness finally got the better of him. Timmy is now a whirlwind of activity, having thrown Cindy to the ground through sheer exuberance once or twice. She says: 'Timmy is a very active fun-loving greyhound. He has had a lot of problems in his life but tries hard to overcome them.'

Timmy

Timothy Timothy, thrown out to roam
Cruel scars on his skin, very wretched and thin
Couldn't sleep in case this place proved not to be home.

Now Timothy Timothy tiddles and tugs
Gnaws people's noses and treads on their toeses
And tosses his toys up and hurries for hugs.

Timothy Timothy frantic for fun:
He gets so excited, unsure what he's bited
Or whether he's frighted, or which thing he's done.

Timothy Timothy no one hurts here.
You're muddled – you've puddled – but you'll still be cuddled
And covered in kisses and never a tear.

Bridgend Dogs' Trust (01656 724 598): 'Mr Tumnus is about six years old and can be temperamental at times. Once he gets to know you he overcomes his grumpiness and likes to cuddle up and bond. When he first came to us he was very worried and reactive but now that he trusts the staff he can be quite sweet — he'll do almost anything for a tasty treat.' He needs an adult-only home with no other dogs, and his new owners would need to be experienced with Staffie-types and to visit Mr T a few times before adopting him.

Mr Tumnus

If you can keep a 'Staff' when all about you
Are leaving theirs out with their wheelie bins,
If you can trust yourself when press men doubt you
Who blame the breed for just a few dogs' sins;
If you can train with firmness that is fitting
And seeing naughty ways still not despair,
Or being heated, don't give way to hitting
As many have been hit beyond repair:

If you can make that Staff see what you're after,
If you can praise, and not just moan and chide,
If you can meet mistrust with love and laughter
And look beyond fear to the good inside;
If you can bear to hear the scorn of others
When you are walking your dog on the lead
And somehow let it meet its doggie brothers
And not let people shame you for its breed:

If you can hear of hoodies who have used them
And hard men who have taught them vicious ways
Yet not blame Staffs for those who would abuse them
And understand a loyal dog obeys:
If you can reach a lost dog's heart and win it
And see this through despite the pain and strife,
Yours is a Staff and all the love that's in it
And – which is more – you'll have a friend for life.

*Apologies to Rudyard Kipling, but he was a great dog
lover, and Staffies like Mr Tumnus need homes.*

Willow

The Lurcher

The bundle of bones was handed in.
It was still a dog, though it could not stand:
A brindle, very young.
It did not know the men in blue
Who took its body in their van
To Lily Lurcher's rescue home.
It did not know or understand
The vet who put it on a drip
Or recognise the steady hand
That pressed its pulse or held its head.
What registered that night
Was that a kind nurse, sitting by
Said that she should not die without a name
So Willow she became;
And Willow's ebbing blood began to flow
And Willow's misty mind began to grasp
And Willow's frame began to fill
Breathing in love of life until
A small abandoned heap of bones
Found out a future bright and new:
A Summerhouse, an owner who adores,
Fine food, fun, fleece beneath her paws.
So Willow may give hope to you:
For if a dog as delicate as she
Could rise up from a bag of bones
To grace us all, what might you be?

I met Willow, now 18 months old and brimming with health, at a gardening gift shop called Summerhouse in Monks Eleigh, where her owner Emma Cook was working. 'Willow had been handed in to Ipswich Police in September 2008, starved almost to the point of death. Covered in fleas and sores and unable to stand because she was so emaciated, she was taken from Lily Lurcher's Rescue Centre to Hadleigh Vet Practice, where a very kind nurse sat with her all night and named her Willow. Now hopefully my beautiful girl has a long happy life ahead of her.'

Willow the Shepherd Cross was discovered in 1999 at Willow Tree Sanctuary in Gainsford End, Essex, and taken to live on a farm in Gosfield by Diana Hulkes. Her dam was 'a little yellow crossbreed' and her sire a very handsome German Shepherd, both inmates at the shelter. Says Diana: 'Dear Willow – a guard till the end. At nine and a half a bit portly, but always game, always ready for a walk and always trusted her vet.'

Willow

The Shepherd Cross

Our guarding girl held her head high
As in her Shepherd eye
A fierce pride burned.
Rose far above her humble caged beginning:
That shelter mating while their backs were turned.

Our guarding girl
Stamped her authority on the farm
Nipping bottoms only if deserving:
Loyal, unswerving, keeping us from harm.

Our guarding girl, her great heart racing
Leaping the ditches with our Labrador
Free as the wind and sky, hunting and chasing
Halcyon days for the shelter dog of yore:
Halcyon days, though numbered now, and dated.

Welcomed the vet, sat on her mat and waited.

Cancer had come for her and chose her blindly.
Young for a Shepherd cross, nine years of age.
Lifted her leg for the soothing shot that kindly
Let out her spirit like the waif from the cage.

Wilson

And, like a rabid lurcher, lean and pale,
Who totters forth, wrapped in a gaudy towel,
Out of her kennel, led by the insane
And drunken wanderings of her feeble brain
The Westie, Rose, arose and gave a burp:
The white and shapeless twerp.

Art thou pale from last night's toot
When thou didst stray into a neighbouring bar
Drinking from some boozer's boot
And claiming to be Streep, the movie star?
Thou art not Meryl, with thy bloodshot eye,
Nor merry neither, now thy brain is dry.

Apologies to Percy Bysshe Shelley but Wilson (Dogs Trust West London branch) needed a home.

The author spotted Wilson's feisty face staring out of the Dogs Trust website gallery of those needing homes, and felt inspired to write an ode on his behalf that reflected his saucy character. The Border Terrier was ten years old when he arrived at Dogs Trust after being picked up as a stray in South West Scotland. Described as 'a cheeky chappie who loves fuss and attention', Wilson has been successfully re-homed and now lives in Luton.

Zak

Zak's a good boy now. No sheep?
I'll round up your chickens. Or your ducks.
How can I please you? I know, I'll do this:
Squeak squeak with my toy
In time to the music. Look, I can do this:
Zigzag, weaving through the sticks
On the obstacle course, racing to retrieve
Two things in my mouth, or three
No matter to me, so long as I can please you.
Master I loved. I was under his feet
In every shed with my Dad.
And when he went to the sky

I kept my eager eye on Mistress for my cues.
Their son, I wait by his hand to run.
Born in Bala, brought up in a storm
I was a bad pup, nipped with needle teeth.
Ashamed, I deserved to lose my home.
They took me to the shelter in a storm again.
So many storms for a young pup to bear.
And I languished there. All the other dogs
Were treasured up and taken but not me.
Nobody wants a biter. So
I bowed my head really low
And let my life away, and didn't care all day.
But then out of despair my people came
And picked me out, and said my name.
Which is why I long to please them.
Bad leg? Ill? Doesn't matter to me
Running through the cloth sausage
Wanting to fetch for Mistress,
Wanting to be brave in the storm
And do no harm. A dog can reform.
A dog can learn. A dog can be reborn.
Zak's a good boy now.

Zak the Collie lived with the Burder family at their homes in Shimpling and Long Melford, Suffolk, where many Border Collies have been treasured over the years. Originally from Wales he became John Burder's favourite dog, and when John passed away Zak looked after widowed Dorothy ('Dot') and their son David. Zak loved games of fetch and squeaked his toys tirelessly, being very clever at obedience and agility work. He recently died of cancer but was a most brave boy – always cheerful and willing to obey. Sadly missed.

No Name

You'll never love me either: let me go
Back to the cast-off kennels whence I came
Back with the losers whining on death row.
Don't even bother giving me a name.
There I shall not be beaten, starved or burned.
There I shall not be scared by hearts of stone.
I can brave out that last shot now I've learned
Nothing awaits me worse than I have known.
Humans are masters. They are Number One.
Dogs must accept their fate and not complain.
Just seven days of grace and I'll be gone:
Never to trouble humankind again.

PART TWO

Adopting a Dog

I want an unwanted dog

THE BRITISH PUBLIC may like to think that, when they abandon their pet dogs by the hundred thousand, they go directly to some sanctuary in the sky where they get free Bonio biscuits and everything is quietly taken care of.

DOG DREGS – THE REALITY

The truth is very different. Here on earth behind the shelter walls, dogs stand in barrack blocks and zinc-lined runs, waiting and hoping, flattening their faces against the bars when they hear human footsteps. And the kennel staff who love them and cannot find them homes get the job of walking the dogs as jauntily as they can and feeding them from charitable donations, or handing them over for their last barbiturate jab – while somewhere far away sit their former owners, blithely oblivious.

The Dogs' Trust estimate that one dog is euthanised in Britain every hour. Last year alone Battersea put down a third of its intake because there was simply no room for them or because they were considered unsuitable for re-homing. Some 8,000 dogs were taken in but 2,815 were destroyed, 1,931 of these healthy dogs. The RSPCA, which no longer accepts abandoned dogs from the public without good reason, destroyed 533 dogs in 2009. Even some of the smaller charities were having up to one-third of their dogs euthanised because nobody wanted them, or because they had been unsuitably bred or unsuitably trained, or not trained at all by irresponsible and cruel owners.

THE STRUGGLING SANCTUARIES

Everywhere in Britain, little sanctuaries struggle to survive, for shamefully animal charities receive no state aid and rely entirely on donations. Government contingency plans for dealing with the next rabies outbreak in the UK show how much we take for granted our network of waif-collecting centres and the dedication of a small band of animal-lovers fighting to make ends meet. I have visited many of the ADCH shelters listed in this book, and many small unaffiliated shelters that are not listed. The cheerful, kind people who run them do so with little thanks or recognition, day in and day out, working like drudges, often for nothing. They are heroes in every sense and this book is dedicated to them. Why do they do it? I've asked them many a time. They all said the same thing.

"Because the dogs are worth it."

Animal welfare work in Britain may draw on a huge reservoir of popular sentimentality, but when you actually turn on the tap, a mere trickle comes out. Only a handful of the sympathetic people do anything to help the dedicated few, yet somewhere among the homes and shelters there may be a future friend of yours, pushing his or her snout through the wire netting, thinking perhaps tomorrow you may come.

These dogs' verses were designed to touch your heart. If they succeeded, and you are now considering giving an unwanted dog a place in your home, please make sure that you have thought it through.

THE RIGHT PEOPLE FOR THE RIGHT REASONS

People who decide on a second-hand dog rather than a new puppy usually do so for the best reasons. They have a settled home where dogs are permitted and which isn't about to be disrupted by a move or a new baby. They can afford the food and expensive vets' bills (the PDSA or People's Dispensary for Sick Animals, which offers free treatment in some areas to the genuinely hard-up, is not an animal National Health Service). They have thought about the mess, the exercise, the grooming, the carpets, the garden, the fences and the time and trouble involved in looking after a four-legged friend for maybe ten to fifteen years, and they realise that a dog is more demanding than a cat or a koi carp.

They have thought about the holidays, and what will happen to the dog when they go away, and they've understood that a dog left alone in the house all day while the owners are at work will often show its anxiety and distress by destruction and barking. The whole family has agreed, including overworked mums and any elderly relatives living at home, that a dog would be welcome, and they have decided where it will be allowed to jump, sit and sleep. And then they have agreed on a rescue dog for its own sake, rather than for what it looks like. They don't just want a fur burglar alarm, a toy or a status symbol. They want a true friend who, once it gets to know its rescuers, will follow them like a shadow, guard them and stand by them through thick and thin.

THE BIG QUESTIONS

So there are a few big questions to ask yourself before you go ahead and adopt a canine waif. The first is: *Do you really want it?* A dog knows no greater anguish than to be abandoned by the owner it loved and a discarded dog has already been through that once. If you think you may be Number Two, please save yourself the trouble.

Secondly, I would advise especial caution if you have young children or grandchildren. Any dog, rescue or not, pure-bred or not, is capable of biting, and small children playing and experimenting with life will often put a pet under the direst pressure while your back is turned. An adult stray from a shelter may have an angelic temperament but it may have been sadistically abused or have ingrained bad habits that will take time and patience to alter. It isn't fair on the child or the dog to expect them to hit it off under these circumstances. Young children cannot read a dog's body language the way grown-ups can. They don't understand where play ends and danger signals begin. This said, many rescue dogs have been successfully homed with children, and the most valuable advice will come from the shelter staff who have had time to get to know the dogs in their care.

There are very few genuinely psychotic dogs that will suddenly bite for no reason at all, but many animals who have suffered great cruelty in the past will snap if they are frightened or pulled about, at least until their confidence in humans is restored. After that you will be able to trust them as you would trust any friend, but do be careful at the outset. Use common sense. The kennel staff will generally know which are the problem customers and they will gladly steer you towards a placid character or a gentle bitch who likes nothing better than kids, kids and yet more kids – as bitches often do. In any case, children must be taught that a dog is not a toy or a squeezebox. Like us, it needs some privacy, rest and respect.

CANINE CASTAWAYS

Last year 107,228 dogs were recorded as abandoned in the UK, an increase of 11% on the previous year. And this figure does *not* include thousands of unwanted racing greyhounds that simply 'go missing' on a yearly basis rather than get recycled through the Retired Greyhound Trust rescue centres. Many of these ex-racers, as rescue campaigners know, have been very cruelly disposed of, and 10,000 bodies were illegally buried in a landfill site in County Durham. A frequent method of execution is with a gun or a bolt-gun. The Greyhound Clinic, Ockendon Kennels in Upminster, offers £30 a head for healthy greyhounds that can be killed for body parts for research, and the trade is condoned by the Royal Veterinary College (I have statements to this effect).

Other canine cast-offs were dropped from bridges, on motorways, in rivers and wheelie-bins – ex-pets, door-mutts, surplus to requirements. Animal welfare workers, sickened by the rising tide, plead for changes in the law and save as many as they can. Still the animal-loving British public rush out to buy more dogs, new dogs, expensive dogs, and the flourishing dog trade produces litter after litter, selling them on the internet to anyone with sufficient cash. The shelters, already bursting at the seams, squeeze in a few more, putting two and even three to a cage, until there is simply no more room at the inn.

During a recession people throw out their dogs like old shoes to save money, so this book has been written to focus people's minds on this emergency and what it really means. Waifs and strays that cannot be found room for end up in vans bound for the local vet's or agency kennels where they have a few days' grace before being quietly destroyed, never to trouble the animal-loving British public again.

Before you go out and buy a new dog, please come to any of the nation's ADCH shelters and look at their second-hand rows. Whether or not you meet a friend, it will bring home to you the enormity of the problem throughout the UK, and the callousness with which other people have shrugged off their responsibilities. You will see faces to amuse you, faces to accuse you and, if you have any feelings at all, faces to break your heart. In the words of Dogs Trust's famous slogan, *A dog is for life, not just for Christmas.*

CHAPTER 2

Where to find one

I F YOU DECIDE ON A RESCUE DOG rather than a new pedigree puppy, you are literally saving a dog's life, because even if the one you choose is not itself on death row, you will be making room at the shelter for another waif who may well have just days to live. Many overcrowded shelters are forced to destroy inmates after the statutory seven days, and now that responsibility for impounding strays has shifted from the police to local authorities, lost souls are kept for the week at council-appointed agencies before being put to sleep. Most of the dogs locked up on Death Row have committed no crime, and there are many affecting cases of animals pleading, in their doggie ways, to live. One mongrel about to be put down at Battersea sat up on his haunches and begged with his paws together. He was reprieved by staff, but few are so lucky. Nobody wants them.

The ADCH (Association of Dogs' and Cats' Homes) is the umbrella organisation that embraces many of the UK and Southern

Ireland's animal charities, shelters and re-homing centres up and down the British Isles. In the list below you will find all the member charities with their phone numbers and email addresses so you can find one or two with branches near you. You can also go on the ADCH website (www.adch.org.uk) for more at-a-glance information. There are many hundreds of ADCH centres and although we have listed many, it would be impractical to try to print all their branch details in this book. Rest assured, there is a centre not far away!

Even if you already know the shelter address do please ring them up or go on their website before you visit, as many animal charities depend on volunteer staff and they are all extremely busy (you might even, if you have any time to spare, consider giving them a hand – they would be desperately grateful). Some of the larger organisations have branches all over the UK, but if you contact any of the listed member charities by phone or visit their websites you can locate a shelter near you and may even be able to see pictures of their dogs currently waiting for homes.

Association of Dogs' and Cats' Homes – Member Charities

MANAGEMENT AND CURRENT MEMBERS

ADCH Presidents	**Organisation**
Nick Blampied	Jersey SPCA
Duncan Green	Margaret Green Animal Rescue

Elected Officers & Committee	**Organisation**
Chairman – Clarissa Baldwin	Dogs Trust
Vice Chairman – Steve Goody	The Blue Cross
Secretary – David Warner	National Animal Welfare Trust
Dennis Baker	Wood Green Animal Shelters
Tony Harris	Gables Farm
Caroline Kisko	The Kennel Club
Nigel Mason	Raystede Centre for Animal Welfare

FULL MEMBERS

Animal Care (Lancaster, Morecombe & District)
Tel: 01524 65495 · *Fax:* 01524 841819 · *Web:* www.animalcarelancaster.co.uk

Animals In Distress
Tel: 01803 812121 · *Fax:* 01803 814 085
Web: www.animalsindistress.uk.com

Ashbourne & District Animal Welfare Society
Tel: 01335 300 494 · *Web:* www.ashbourneanimalwelfare.org

Assisi Animal Sanctuary
Tel: 02891 812622 · *Web:* www.assisi.dnet.co.uk

Bath Dogs & Cats Homes
Tel: 01225 787321· *Fax:* 01225 311118
Web: www.bathcatsanddogshome.org.uk

Battersea Dogs & Cats Home
Tel: 020 7627 9203/4 · *Fax:* 020 7627 9200 www.dogshome.org

Birmingham Dogs' Home
Tel: 01902 790618 (SS) · *Tel:* 0121 643 5211 (BDH) · *Fax:* 0121 6430910 (BDH)
Web: www.birminghamdogshome.org.uk

The Blue Cross
Tel: 01993 822651· *Fax:* 01993 823083 · *Web:* www.bluecross.org.uk

The Animals' Refuge, Carlisle
Tel: 01228 560 082 · *Web:* www.animalrefuge.co.uk

Bolton Destitute Animal's Shelter
Tel: 01204 526486 · *Web:* www.animalshelter.org.uk

Border Collie Trust GB
Tel: 0871 560 2282 · *Web:* www.bordercollietrustgb.org.uk

Cork Animal Care Society
Tel: 00 353 214551781 · *Web:* www.animalcaresociety.ie

Dogs Trust
Tel: 020 7837 0006 · *Fax:* 020 7833 2701 · *Web:* www.dogstrust.org.uk

Dublin SPCA
Tel: 00 353 14935502 · *Web:* www.dspca.ie

Dumfries & Galloway Canine Rescue Centre
Tel: 01387 770210 · *Web:* www.caninerescue.co.uk

Eden Animal Rescue
Tel: 01931 716114 · *Web:* www.edenanimalrescue.org.uk

Edinburgh Dog and Cat Home
Tel: 0131 669 5331 · *Fax:* 0131 657 5601 · *Web:* www.edch.org.uk

English Springer Spaniel Welfare
Tel: 01752 691579 · *Web:* www.englishspringerwelfare.co.uk

Fen Bank Greyhound Rescue
Tel: 01205 270166 · *Web:* www.fenbankgreyhounds.co.uk

Foal Farm Animal Rescue Centre
Tel: 01959 572 386 · *Web:* www.foalfarm.org.uk

Gables Farm Dogs' and Cats' Home (Plymouth)
Tel: 01752 331 602 · *Fax:* 01752 331 604 · *Web:* www.gablesfarm.org.uk

**Gloucestershire Animal Welfare Association
and Cheltenham Animal Shelter**
Tel: 0871 223 0404 · *Fax:* 01242 523676 · *Web:* www.gawa.org.uk

Greyhound Rescue West of England
Tel: 07000 785092 · *Web:* www.grwe.com

Guernsey SPCA
Tel: 01481 257261 · *Fax:* 01481 251 147 · *Web:* www.gspca.org.gg

Holly Hedge Animal Sanctuary
Tel: 01275 474719 · *Web:* www.hollyhedge.org.uk

**HULA Animal Rescue (Bedfordshire Home
for unwanted and lost animals)**
Tel: 01908 584000 · *Fax:* 01908 282020 · *Web:* www.hularescue.org

ISPCA
Tel: 00353 43 25029 · *Fax:* 00353 43 25024 · *Web:* www.ispca.ie

Jersey SPCA Animals' Shelter
Tel: 01534 724 331 · *Fax:* 01534 871797 · *Web:* www.jspca.org.je

Jerry Green Dog Rescue
Tel: 01652 657820 · *Web:* www.jerrygreendogs.org.uk

The Kennel Club
Tel: 0870 6066750 · *Fax:* 020 7518 1028 · *Web:* www.thekennelclub.org.uk

The Labrador Lifeline Trust
Tel: 01252 849560/07860 691251 · *Web:* www.labrador-lifeline.co.uk

Leicester Animal Aid
Tel/Fax: 01455 888 257 · *Tel only*: 01455 888 55
Web: www.leicesteranimalaid.org.uk

Leitrim Animal Welfare
Tel: 00 353 71964 8300 · *Web:* www.leitrimanimals.com

Lord Whisky Sanctuary Fund
Tel: 01303 862 622 · *Web:* www.lordwhisky.co.uk

Manchester & Cheshire Dogs Homes
Tel: 0871 918 1212 · *Fax:* 0161 277 6949 · *Web:* www.dogshome.net

Manx SPCA
Tel: 01624 851 672 · Tel/*Fax:* 01624 852 923 · *Web:* www.mspca.im

Margaret Green Animal Rescue
Tel: 01929 480 474 · *Fax:* 01929 480860
Web: www.margaretgreenanimalrescue.org.uk

Mayhew Animal Home
Tel: 020 8969 0178/7110 · *Fax:* 020 8964 3221
Web: www.mayhewanimalhome.org

National Animal Welfare Trust
Tel: 020 8950 0177 · *Fax:* 020 8420 4454 · *Web:* www.nawt.org.uk

Newcastle Dog and Cat Shelter
Tel: 0191 215 0435 · *Fax:* 0191 266 9942 · *Web:* www.dogandcatshelter.com

North Clwyd Animal Rescue
Tel: 01745 560546 · *Web:* www.ncar.org.uk

North Shore Animal League International
Tel: 01206 274058 · *Fax:* 01206 273400 · *Web:* www.nsali.org

PAWS (Ireland)
Tel: 052 53507 · *Web:* www.paws.ie

Porthcawl Animal Welfare Society
Tel: 01656 773307 · *Web:* www.pawsporthcawl.com

Raystede Centre for Animal Welfare
Tel: 01825 840 252 · *Fax:* 01825 840 995 · *Web:* www.raystede.org

Retired Greyhound Trust
Tel: 0844 826 8424 · *Fax:* 0844 826 8425
Web: www.retiredgreyhounds.co.uk

RSPCA
Tel: 0300 123 0365 · *Web:* www.rspca.org.uk

RSPCA Liverpool Branch
Tel: 0151 220 3812 · *Fax:* 0151 220 3821
Web: www.rspcaliverpoolbranch.co.uk

Scottish SPCA
Tel: 0131 339 5602 · *Fax:* 0131 339 4777 · *Web:* www.scottishspca.org

Society for Abandoned Animals
Tel: 0161 9735318 · *Web:* www.saarescue.co.uk

St Francis Home For Animals (Newquay)
Tel: 01637 872976 · *Web:* www.stfrancisfourcanines.co.uk

Stokenchurch Dog Rescue
Tel: 0482695 · *Web:* www.stokenchurchdogrescue.co.uk

Teckels Animal Sanctuaries
Tel: 01452 740 300 · *Web:* www.teckels.org

USPCA
Tel: 028 90814242 · *Fax:* 028 93373919 · *Web:* www.uspca.co.uk

Wood Green Animal Shelters
Tel: 0844 248 8181 · *Fax:* 01480 832815 · *Web:* www.woodgreen.org.uk

Woodside Animal Welfare Trust
Tel: 01752 347503 · *Web:* www.woodsidesanctuary.org.uk

ASSOCIATE MEMBERS

Airedale Terrier Club of Scotland
Tel: 01241 830 406 · *Web:* www.atcsonline.co.uk

Animals in Need
Tel: 0151 549 0959 · *Web:* www.animals-in-need.co.uk

Ardley Rescue Kennels
Tel: 01869 346 307 · *Web:* www.ardleyrescuekennels.co.uk

Babbington Rescue CIC
Tel: 0115 932 4576 · *Web:* www.babbington-rescue.org.uk

Barnsley Animal Rescue Charity
Tel: 01226 742 950 · *Web:* www.barnsleyanimalrescue.org.uk

The Beagle Welfare Scheme
Tel: 01260 223 057 · *Web:* www.beagleadvice.org.uk

Boxer Welfare Scotland
Tel: 01779 812 799 · *Web:* www.boxerwelfarescotland.co.uk

Coventry Cat Group
Tel: 02476 268 703 · *Web:* www.coventrycatgroup.org.uk

Freshfields Animal Rescue
Tel: 0151 931 1604 · *Web:* www.freshfieldsrescue.org.uk

Give a Greyhound a Home (GAGAH)
Tel: 01771 644 059 · *Web:* www.gagah.co.uk

Great Dane Adoption Society
Tel: 01205 481 248 · *Web:* www.danes.org.uk

Greyhound Welfare
Tel: 01633 892 846 · *Web:* www.greyhoundwelfare.org.uk

GSD 2000 Rescue & Re-home
Tel: 01242 680 052 · *Web:* www.gsd2000.com

Labrador Rescue Kent & Borders
Tel: 01634 666 419 · *Web:* www.labrescuekent.co.uk

Labrador Welfare
Tel: 0114 266 1756 · *Web:* www.labradorwelfare.org

Oldies Club
Tel: 08445 868 656 · *Web:* www.oldies.org.uk

Rain Rescue
Tel: 07946 618 011 · *Web:* www.rainrescue.co.uk

Rottweiler Welfare Association
Tel: 01491 652 105 · *Web:* www.rottweilerwelfare.co.uk

Valgrays Border Collie & Animal Rescue
Tel: 01883 624 513 · *Web:* www.valgraysbcrescue.org.uk

West Cork Animal Welfare Group
Tel: 00 353 86 850 0131 · *Web:* www.westcorkanimals.com

DOGS TRUST RE-HOMING CENTRES

Head office: 17 Wakley Street, London EC1V 7RQ
Tel: 020 7837 0006 · *Web:* www.dogstrust.org.uk
Email:info@dogstrust.org.uk
Registered charity numbers: 227523 and SCO37843

Branches:

Ballymena, Co. Antrim. *Tel:* 028 2565 2977
Bridgend, Mid Glamorgan. *Tel:* 01656 725 219
Canterbury, Kent. *Tel:* 01227 792 505
Darlington, Co. Durham. *Tel:* 01325 333114
Dublin, Ireland. *Tel:* 00 353 187 91000
Evesham, Worcs. *Tel:* 01386 830 613
Glasgow, Scotland. *Tel:* 0141 773 5130
Ilfracombe, North Devon. *Tel:* 01271 812 709

Kenilworth, Warks. *Tel:* 01926 484 398
Leeds, West Yorks. *Tel:* 0113 281 4920
Merseyside, Liverpool. *Tel:* 0151 480 0660
Newbury, Berks. *Tel:* 01488 658 391
Roden, Shrops. *Tel:* 01952 770 225
Salisbury, Wilts. *Tel:* 01980 629 634
Shoreham, West Sussex. *Tel:* 01273 452 576
Snetterton, Norfolk. *Tel:* 01953 498 377
West Calder, Edinburgh. *Tel:* 01506 873 459
West London, Uxbridge. *Tel:* 0845 076 3647

WOOD GREEN ANIMAL SHELTERS

Godmanchester Shelter (HQ)
Kings Bush Farm, London Road, Godmanchester, Cambs, PE29 2NH
Tel: 0844 248 8181
Dogs at main centre only

BLUE CROSS (DOG) ADOPTION CENTRES

Bromsgrove
Wildmoor Lane, Catshill, Bromsgrove, Worcs B61 0RJ
Tel: 0121 453 3130

Burford
Shilton Road, Burford, Oxon OX18 4PF
Tel: 01993 822483

Felixstowe
333 High Street, Walton, Felixstowe, Suffolk IP11 9QL
Tel: 01394 283254

Hertfordshire
Kimpton Bottom, Herts SG4 8EU
Tel: 01438 832232

Lewknor
London Road, Lewknor, Oxon OX49 5RY
Tel: 01844 355293

Northiam
St Francis Fields, Northiam, E. Sussex TN31 6LP
Tel: 01797 252243

Southampton
Bubb Lane, West End, Southampton, Hants SO30 2HL
Tel: 023 8069 2894

Thirsk
Parklands, Station Road, Topcliffe, Thirsk, N. Yorks YO7 3SE
Tel: 01845 577759

Tiverton
Chilton Gate, Bickleigh, Tiverton, Devon EX16 8RS
Tel: 01884 855291

BREED RESCUE VIA THE KENNEL CLUB

For information on particular breeds available for re-homing, please visit
the website of the Kennel Club Online Services (www.the-kennel-
club.org.uk) where you will find a list of over 200 individual breeds with
rescue organisations and their contact details. At the touch of a button you
may also be able to locate a particular pedigree dog of your choice in need
of adoption. If you don't have access to the internet you can phone: 0844
463 3980.

RETIRED GREYHOUND TRUST RE-HOMING CENTRES

EAST OF ENGLAND
East Anglia
Tel: 01406 330459 · *Web:* www.kamascave.com

Eastern Counties
Tel: 08456 022658 · *Web:* http://norfolk.retiredgreyhounds.co.uk/

Greyhoundhomer RGT Suffolk
Tel: 01473 659866 · *Web:* www.greyhoundhomer.org.uk

Mildenhall, Suffolk & East Cambs
Tel: 01638 716578 · *Web:* http://mildenhall.retiredgreyhounds.co.uk/

Peterborough – Brambleberry
Tel: 07843 655003 · *Web:* www.brambleberry-greyhounds.co.uk

Peterborough Greyhound Welfare
Tel: 07737 683969 · *Web:* http://peterborough.retiredgreyhounds.co.uk/

Peterborough RGT
Tel: 01832 205363 · *Web:* http://greyhounds24-7.retiredgreyhounds.co.uk/

West Norfolk
Tel: 07767 362248 · *Web:* http://westnorfolk.retiredgreyhounds.co.uk/

Wisbech
Tel: 01945 430311 · *Web:* http://wisbech.retiredgreyhounds.co.uk/

Yarmouth (Homefinders)
Tel: 0845 4583797 · *Web:* www.yarmouthstadium.co.uk/homefinders.htm

EAST MIDLANDS
East Midlands
Tel: 01636 822032 · *Web:* www.rgtmidlands.co.uk

Leicestershire
Tel: 01664 812361 · *Web:* http://leicestershire.retiredgreyhounds.co.uk/

Lincolnshire
Tel: 01522 569825 · *Web:* www.lincolnshiregreyhoundtrust.com

Northampton
Tel: 01604 832742 · *Web:* www.northantsgreyhoundrescue.co.uk

Nottingham
Tel: 0115 9533344 · *Web:* www.rgtnottingham.org.uk/

Worksop
Tel: 01909 724901

LONDON/SOUTH EAST
Brighton & Hove RGT
Tel: 01444 881788 · *Web:* http://brighton.retiredgreyhounds.co.uk/

Essex – Basildon
Tel: 01268 415716 · *Web:* http://basildon.retiredgreyhounds.co.uk/

Essex – Brentwood
Tel: 01277 373799 · *Web:* http://brentwood.retiredgreyhounds.co.uk/

Essex – Greyhoundhomer RGT
Tel: 01708 551 689 · *Web:* www.greyhoundhomer.co.uk

Essex – Harlow
Tel: 01279 793752 · *Web:* www.harlowhounds.org

Essex – Maldon (Clarks Farm)
Tel: 01621 788315 · *Web:* www.clarksfarmgreyhounds.ik.com

Essex – Romford (RGOA)
Tel: 01708 640895 · *Web:* www.rgoa.org.uk

Essex – Walthamstow
Tel: 01992 890540 · *Web:* www.wsretiredgreyhounds.co.uk

Essex - Walthamstow/Henlow
Tel: 02084 449649 · *Web:* www.wkretiredgreyhounds.co.uk

Greyhound Lifeline RGT (Hants/Berks)
Tel: 07828 138378 · *Web:* www.greyhoundlifeline.co.uk

Hertfordshire – Greyhoundhomer RGT
Tel: 01279 501 899 · *Web:* www.greyhoundhomer.co.uk

Isle of Wight
Tel: 07933 785696

Jersey
Tel: 01534 742619 · *Web:* www.greyrescue.co.uk

Kent – Croftview Rehoming Kennels
Tel: 01474 815273 · *Web:* /www.rgtcroftview.co.uk

Kent – Sittingbourne RGT
Tel: 01227 722847 · *Web:* www.rgtsittingbourne.co.uk

London – Wimbledon (SW)
Tel: 01932 224918 · *Web:* www.hershamhounds.org

Portsmouth
Tel: 01730 893255 · *Web:* www.portsmouthretiredgreyhounds.org

RGT Head Office
Tel: 0844 826 8424 · *Web:* www.retiredgreyhounds.co.uk/

Southampton
Tel: 02380 619225

WEST MIDLANDS
Birmingham – Hall Green
Tel: 01214 264810 · *Web:* www.hallgreenrgt.co.uk

Birmingham – Perry Barr
Tel: 01217 827702 · *Web:* www.rgtperrybarr.co.uk

Birmingham – Thistle Grove
Tel: 01926 632423 · *Web:* www.greyhoundtrust.co.uk

Oxford
Tel: 01865 374792 · *Web:* http://oxford.retiredgreyhounds.co.uk/

Rugby & Coventry
Tel: 01788 833855 · *Web:* www.watchkennelsrgt.co.uk

Shropshire and Borders
Tel: 01743 872395 · *Web:* http://shropshire.retiredgreyhounds.co.uk/

Wolverhampton – Monmore
Tel: 01922 412212 · *Web:* www.rgtwolverhampton.co.uk

Worcester
Tel: 01299 861514

NORTH WEST
Cumbria
Tel: 01900 872776 · *Web:* http://workington.retiredgreyhounds.co.uk/

Cumbria (South Lakes)
Tel: 015395 52394 · *Web:* www.ourgreyhounds.co.uk/

Manchester
Tel: 01524 852784 · *Web:* http://manchester.retiredgreyhounds.co.uk

Manchester – Belle Vue
Tel: 07778 664501 · *Web:* www.bellevuergt.co.uk

Merseyside
Tel: 01925 638858 · *Web:* www.adoptagreyhound.co.uk

North West – Cheshire & Wirral
Tel: 07925 384 477 · *Web:* www.northwestrgt.com

Sheffield
Tel: 01142 888300 · *Web:* www.sheffieldretiredgreyhounds.co.uk

West Yorkshire – Huddersfield & Wakefield
Tel: 01924 848121 · *Web:* http://westyorkshire.retiredgreyhounds.co.uk/

NORTH EAST

Bridlington
Tel: 01262 609343 · *Web:* http://bridlington.retiredgreyhounds.co.uk/

Durham – Hollin Hall
Tel: 07876077093 · *Web:* http://hollinhall.retiredgreyhounds.co.uk/

Durham – Pelaw Grange
Tel: 01325 360197 · *Web:* http://pelawgrange.retiredgreyhounds.co.uk/

East Riding
Tel: 01482 503944 · *Web:* http://eastriding.retiredgreyhounds.co.uk/

Hartlepool
Tel: 01429 260256 · *Web:* http://hartlepool.retiredgreyhounds.co.uk/

Hull
Tel: 01482 223228 · *Web:* http://hull.retiredgreyhounds.co.uk/

North Yorkshire
Tel: 01609 761014 · *Web:* http://northyorkshire.retiredgreyhounds.co.uk/

North-East
Tel: 01207 299311 · *Web:* http://north-east.retiredgreyhounds.co.uk/

Northumberland
Tel: 01434 673804 · *Web:* http://northumberland.retiredgreyhounds.co.uk/

SCOTLAND
Borders
Tel: 07967 057759 · *Web:* http://borders.retiredgreyhounds.co.uk/

Edinburgh
Tel: 01314 760069

Glasgow – Shawfield
Tel: 01292 263493 · *Web:* www.shawfieldrgt.co.uk

Isle of Skye
Tel: 01470 511705 · *Web:* www.rgt-skye.co.uk

West Lothian
Tel: 01501 753224 · *Web:* www.rgt-westlothian.co.uk

WALES/SOUTH WEST

Bristol
Tel: 01454 632333 · *Web:* www.freewebs.com/southwestsighthounds/

Cornwall
Tel: 01872 560 629 · *Web:* http://cornwall.retiredgreyhounds.co.uk/

Devon (East) – Honiton
Tel: 01404 861160 · *Web:* www.rgthillview.co.uk/

Dorset & Somerset
Tel: 01823 480835 · *Web:* http://dorset.retiredgreyhounds.co.uk/

Dorset (Poole)
Tel: 01747 854042 · *Web:* http://dorset-poole.retiredgreyhounds.co.uk/

Morwenstow (Cornwall & Devon)
Tel: 01288 331725 · *Web:* http://morwenstow.retiredgreyhounds.co.uk/

North Cornwall & West Devon
Tel: 01288 352656 · *Web:* http://northcornwall.retiredgreyhounds.co.uk/

SW England (Homesafe)
Tel: 01624 861408

Swindon
Tel: 01793 721253 · *Web:* http://swindon.retiredgreyhounds.co.uk/

Wales (South)
Tel: 01633 892846 · *Web:* www.greyhoundsinwales.moonfruit.com

Wales (West)
Tel: 01554 773136 · *Web:* http://westwales.retiredgreyhounds.co.uk/

RSPCA BRANCHES AND RE-HOMING CENTRES

For further information see the RSPCA website: www.rspca.org.uk

RSPCA Ashley Heath Animal Centre
Horton Road, Ashley Heath, Ringwood, Hampshire BH24 2ET
Tel: 0300 123 0749

RSPCA Birmingham Animal Centre
Barnes Hill, Weoley Castle, Birmingham B29 5UP
Tel: 0300 123 0754

RSPCA Blackberry Farm Animal Centre
Quainton, Aylesbury, Buckinghamshire. HP22 4RJ
Tel: 0300 123 0752

RSPCA Block Fen Animal Centre
Block Fen Drove, Wimblington, Cambridgeshire PE15 0FB
Tel: 0300 123 0726

RSPCA Bryn-y-Maen Animal Centre
Bryn-y-Maen, Upper Colwyn Bay, Clwyd LL28 5EJ
Tel: 0300 123 0745

RSPCA Felledge Farm Animal Centre
Waldridge Lane, Chester Moor, Chester-Le-Street, Co. Durham DH2 3RX
Tel: 0300 123 0724

RSPCA Gonsal Farm Animal Centre
Dorrington, Shrewsbury, Shropshire SY5 7ET
Tel: 0300 123 0753

RSPCA Great Ayton Animal Centre
Yarm Lane, Great Ayton, Nr Middlesbrough, Cleveland TS9 6QB
Tel: 0300 123 074

RSPCA Leybourne Animal Centre
199 Castle Way, Leybourne, West Malling, Kent ME19 5HW
Tel: 0300 123 0751

RSPCA Millbrook Animal Centre
Guildford Road, Chobham, Surrey GU24 8EH
Tel: 0300 123 0740

RSPCA Newport Animal Centre
Hartridge Farm Road, Ringland Way, Newport, Gwent NP6 2LL
Tel: 0300 123 0744

RSPCA South Godstone Animal Centre
Eastbourne Road, South Godstone, Surrey RH9 8JB
Tel: 0300 123 0741

RSPCA Southridge Animal Centre
Packhorse Lane, Ridge, Potters Bar, Hertfordshire EN6 3LZ
Tel: 0300 123 0704

RSPCA West Hatch Animal Centre
West Hatch, Taunton , Somerset TA3 5RT
Tel: 0300 123 0747

RSPCA BRANCH ANIMAL CENTRES

RSPCA Bath & District Branch
Bath Cats and Dogs Home, The Avenue, Claverton Down, Bath BA2 7AZ
Tel: 01225 787321

RSPCA Blackpool/North Lancs Branch
Longview Kennels, Division Lane, Marton, Blackpool FY4 5EB
Tel: 01253 763991

RSPCA Bradford & District Branch
Animals Home & Clinic, Mount Street (off Leeds Road), Bradford BD3 9SW
Tel: 01274 723063

RSPCA Bristol & District Branch
Bristol Dogs Home, 50 Albert Road, St Phillips, Bristol BS2 0XW
Tel: 01179 776043

RSPCA Burton-on-Trent Branch
Animal Home, Hillfield Lane, Stretton, Burton-on-Trent DE13 0BN
Tel: 01283 569165

RSPCA Bury, Oldham & District Branch
Animal Centre, 21a Rhodes Bank, Oldham, Lancashire OL1 1UA
Tel: 0161 6244725

RSPCA Chesterfield & North Derbyshire Branch
Chesterfield Animal Centre, 137 Spital Lane, Chesterfield S41 0HL
Tel: 01246 273358

RSPCA Cornwall Branch
The William & Patricia Venton, RSPCA Cornwall Branch Animal Centre,
Higher Quoit, St Columb, Cornwall TR9 6JS
Tel: 01637 881455

RSPCA Coventry & District Branch
Brownshill Green Farm, Coundon Wedge Drive, Allesley, Coventry CV5 9DQ
Tel: 02476 336616

RSPCA Derby & District Branch
45 Abbey Street, Derby DE22 3SP
Tel: 01332 344620

RSPCA Doncaster, Rotherham & District Branch
RSPCA South Yorkshire Animal Centre, Black Firs Farm, Great North Road,
Bawtry , South Yorkshire DN10 6DE
Tel: 01302 719790

RSPCA Dorset West Branch
RSPCA Taylor's Animal Rehoming Centre, Higher Dairy, Kingston Maurward
College , Dorchester, Dorset DT2 8PY
Tel: 01305 259672

RSPCA Essex Trust
RSPCA Danaher Animal Home for Essex, Thorley Farm, Hedingham Road,
Wethersfield, Nr Braintree , Essex CM7 4EQ
Tel: 01371 851201

RSPCA Exeter, East & West Devon Branch
RSPCA Little Valley Animal Shelter, Black Hat Lane, Bakers Hill, Exeter EX2 9TA
Tel: 01392 439898

RSPCA Halifax, Huddersfield & District Branch
Wade Street, Halifax , Yorkshire . HX1 1SN
Tel: 01422 365628

RSPCA Hull & East Riding Branch
Animal Centre, Clough Road, Hull , East Yorkshire HU6 7PE
Tel: 01482 341331

RSPCA Isle of Wight Branch
RSPCA Godshill Animal Centre, Bohemia Corner, Godshill, Isle of Wight PO38 3NA
Tel: 01983 840287

RSPCA Kent – Isle of Thanet Branch
East Kent Animal Centre, Queensdown Road, Woodchurch, Birchington, Kent CT7 0HG
Tel: 01843 826180

RSPCA Lancashire East Branch
Nearer Holker House Farm, Altham, Huncoat, Accrington , Lancashire BB5 5UU
Tel: 01254 231118

RSPCA Leicestershire Branch
RSPCA Woodside Animal Centre, 190 Scudamore Road, Leicester LE3 1UQ
Tel: 01162 336677

RSPCA Liverpool Branch
Halewood Animal Centre, Higher Road, Halewood, Liverpool L26 9TX
Tel: 0151 486 1706

RSPCA Llys Nini Branch
Penllergaer, Swansea, West Glamorgan SA4 1WB
Tel: 01792 229345

RSPCA North Somerset Branch
RSPCA Brent Knoll Animal Centre, Brent Knoll, Nr Burnham-on-Sea,
Somerset TA9 4BC
Tel: 01278 782671

RSPCA Norwich & Mid Norfolk Branch
PAWS Centre, 71–75 Barrack Street, Norwich NR3 1WJ
Tel: 01603 766001

RSPCA Nottingham Trust
RSPCA Animal Shelter, Nottingham Road, Radcliffe-on-Trent,
Nottinghamshire NG12 2DW
Tel: 01159 334422

RSPCA Preston & District Branch
Slack Cottage, Ribbleton Avenue, Preston, Lancashire PR2 6QL
Tel: 01772 792553

RSPCA Rochdale & District Branch
RSPCA Roch Valley Animal Centre, 1 Redcross Street, Rochdale, Lancashire
OL12 0NZ
Tel: 01706 861897

RSPCA Sheffield Branch
RSPCA Sheffield Animal Centre, 2 Stadium Way, Sheffield S9 3HN
Tel: 01142 898050

RSPCA Solent Branch
RSPCA The Stubbington Ark , 174–176 Ranvilles Lane, Fareham, Hampshire
PO14 3EZ
Tel: 01329 667541

RSPCA Southport, Birkdale & District Branch
RSPCA Animal Home, New Cut Lane, Birkdale, Southport PR8 3DW
Tel: 01704 567624

RSPCA Suffolk East & Ipswich Branch
Martlesham Animal Home , 2 Mill Lane, Martlesham, Woodbridge, Suffolk
IP12 4PD
Tel: 01473 623280

RSPCA Sussex Brighton & East Grinstead Branch
RSPCA Brighton Animal Centre, Braypool Lane, Patcham, Brighton BN1 8ZH
Tel: 01273 554218

RSPCA Sussex – Chichester & District Branch
RSPCA Mount Noddy Animal Centre, Black Mill Lane, Crockerhill, Eartham,
Nr Chichester, West Sussex PO18 0LL
Tel: 01243 773359

RSPCA Warrington, Halton & St Helens Branch
RSPCA Animal Centre , Slutchers Lane, Bank Quay, Warrington WA1 1NA
Tel: 01925 632944

RSPCA Wirral & Chester Branch
RSPCA Wirral Animal Centre, Cross Lane, Wallasey , Merseyside CH45 8RH
Tel: 0151 638 6318

RSPCA Yorkshire – York & District Branch
RSPCA Animal Home, Landing Lane, Clifton, York YO2 4RH
Tel: 01904 654949

CHAPTER 3

Practicalities

VACCINE COMPLIANCE

HOW MUCH DOES IT COST?

So far as costs are concerned, the rescue dog is a bargain. Not only do most British dogs' homes check the animal's health and temperament for you, but they will take back any dog that proves unsuitable. You won't get a fairer deal than that from a pedigree breeder.

How much do the shelters charge? It varies from a suitable donation to a couple of hundred pounds (again you can get this information by ringing the charity itself). Many animal homes run on a shoestring and must therefore ask you to help with 'the ones left behind'. Besides, these dogs have already been cast off once as valueless. If they were simply given away free, what chance of the same thing happening again? Compare what these charities ask with what breeders may charge you for a puppy – anything up to £1,500 and even beyond – and you get some idea what a good deal this is.

Sometimes the charity officially retains ownership of the dog, should anything unforeseen happen to prevent you from looking after it in the future. Some of the larger charities are able to run a visiting system, with someone to give advice, do a home check and see how the new family member is settling in. Inexperienced dog owners find this a tremendous help, although not all shelters can afford to do it.

DISEASES AND VACCINATION

Some people who write pedigree dog books are fond of warning readers not to adopt a rescue dog. They say these 'rejects' must be either dangerous or diseased and that you should only ever get a puppy from a pedigree breeder. *Rubbish!* say all the owners of our Doggerel dogs. Getting a waif from a shelter has brought as much joy and love to the rescuers as spending a king's ransom on a pure-bred puppy. As to the risk of disease, all the larger charity shelters I've visited gave their dogs a medical check-up before they let them out and vaccinated them against the major diseases. Those with manageable numbers even wormed, bathed and deflea-ed them as well. There is always the chance of infection between animals crowded together, whether it be in a fastidious shelter, a show or a vet's waiting room, and staff at dogs' homes realise the risks and take every possible precaution, watching for signs of incubated disease on their premises. Canine parvovirus broke out, not in these charity homes, but at pedigree shows and kennels.

Please take your new adopted dog, whether pup or adult, to the local vet and he or she will advise you on vaccination for your area, but phone beforehand, explaining where the animal comes from and roughly how old it is. If it's a puppy, it should be carried or taken by car; if it's an adult and too big to carry, the vet will advise you on the phone what to do. In these circumstances some prefer to make a house call, to save you walking the streets with an uninoculated dog and sitting in their waiting room. (If you don't know of a local vet, look on the internet or in the Yellow Pages.) All dogs need protection against the killer diseases and the larger rescue organisations will arrange initial vaccination themselves. Survival of the fittest is all very well unless your particular dog happens not to be the fittest, and you should be on his or her side should nature call them to account. Never take an uninoculated dog out and about until its vaccination is complete. A puppy is utterly vulnerable and an adult dog transported to a new area runs a high risk of infection. Rescue dogs are not expensive. The least you can do is to pay for a course of vaccination for the poor little devil.

The major dog killers in the UK are distemper (and hardpad), infectious canine hepatitis (also known as viral hepatitis and nothing to do with the human version), leptospirosis and canine parvovirus. Distemper, a frequently fatal viral disease, is signalled early on by fever, listlessness and lack of appetite, as well as vomiting. These signs may be followed by coughing, yellow discharge from the nose and eyes, thickening of the skin and footpads, and convulsions. The disease is airborne and even if a dog recovers, he may have infected other dogs and be left with incurable tremors all his life. A couple of jabs will see your dog or puppy through all these dangerous diseases for the first year and thereafter you should consult your vet on the necessity of boosters. Some authorities now question the need for top-up vaccinations and research has emerged on certain health risks associated with them. Please do your homework and find out about this – as the dog's owner it will be your responsibility and finally your decision.

Canine hepatitis is a liver disease; leptospirosis has two forms, one of which attacks the kidneys; and canine parvovirus (the name means 'little virus') is a comparatively new form of enteritis that can kill without showing any symptoms at all. In North America and the European continent, of course, rabies vaccination is required by law, and now that we can take dogs abroad with a pet passport, canine globetrotters must get their shots just like human travellers. When I was visiting the shelters researching my other dog books (I've written five earlier ones), pups in kennels and shelters would often, to save expense, be given a 'measles' vaccination against distemper to tide them over. You should ask about this and whether you may have a certificate for your vet's reference.

Vaccination will cost you something (the PDSA do *not* offer it free). But you should think of this as part of the purchase price of your pet.

CHOOSING ONE TO SUIT YOU

Of course you don't have to choose *one* at all: two that have been kennelled together may be lifelong pals and will often help each other settle in. If they are of opposite sexes, of course, one would need to be neutered, and you should also think in terms of which dog will be 'in charge': animals are not democratic and if there is any doubt about their status they tend to fight. A difference in size or age will help them make up their minds.

The choice of pup or adult, male or female, large or small, smooth or shaggy, will depend entirely on you and your family set-up. What can you handle? The most popular choices *are the easiest to re-home*. The more unlovely, scraggy, elderly and miserable a dog looks, the slimmer its chances of impressing anyone. It will probably skulk in the corner or stare out from its plastic bed, knowing its doggie days are numbered. If you don't have children, you might consider one of these despondent wrecks. They may not like you at all at first; they may not eat; they may hide behind the sofa. But as you can see from the doggies herein versed, they can come out like stars and bluebells, with a little patience.

PUPS

Pups are notoriously cuddly. This is a trick of nature to get you to take them home, where they will go through a wetting and messing stage, followed by a teething and tearing stage. Try to look at the pup as a would-be dog and you'll get the picture. It may be intending to grow into something unusual, and today's large-footed babe may be tomorrow's behemoth. Rescue pups are often kennelled with their mother, so you can see at least half of what you'll get.

Pups have a socialising period between four and 14 weeks, and the ideal time to adopt is around seven to nine weeks. Before that, they need contact with their littermates or they may grow up unsure of other dogs, and if it's later, they may have problems adjusting to people. A pup should be picked up carefully, using both hands, and cradled gently. Many dog tots are badly injured by being dropped, and children are often the droppers. A healthy pup is wriggly, soft and plump. Its skin is loose and mobile and flops back into place. There should be no discharge from eyes or nose: frothy milk down the nose may be a sign of a cleft palate. Coughs and sneezes indicate more than a cold, and pop-eyes are a bad sign too. Ears should be clean and not smelly; teeth should clench perfectly and gums should be pink, not anaemic-looking. Little thighs should be free from spots and scabs; black specs in the fur mean flea-dirt, and signs of diarrhoea mean trouble. Tums should have no lumps or bumps: umbilical hernias require a minor operation. Limbs should be strong rather than rickety. Beware of adopting a cold, skinny pup, unless you are prepared for it to die on you.

A bloated appearance, though, simply means worms, and you should have the puppy wormed by a vet in any case. Roundworms such as *toxocara canis* (about which we have all heard so much) look like pieces of pinkish cotton or string, 5 to 15 cm long and coiled like a spring. They may cause coughing, vomiting and diarrhoea in pups, and the eggs may cause an extremely rare disease called *toxocariasis* in children if they ingest infected soil. Tell children to wash their hands after playing with pups (or soil) and make sure your pet is given appropriate doses of worming tablets from the vet.

There is another common parasite found in dogs – the tapeworm, which is flat like a piece of tape and attaches to the dog's bowel by little stickers. Small segments like rice grains or melon seeds break off and are deposited on the ground. Tapeworms are usually associated with one of their hosts, the flea, so if you see signs of either ask the vet to prescribe a little something. Tapeworms may cause listlessness and loss of appetite in a pup but may be symptomless. Parasitic worms, by the way, are common in mammals. Cats have their own and so do we – threadworms, found in children, are nothing to do with pets.

ADULTS

Rescue dogs of all ages come in every shape and size. Age can be roughly determined by tooth discolouration, although this may also be due to illness. Yellowish brown stains and bluntness of the canines usually mean the dog is over five years old, unless it smokes a pipe. Dogs do go grey like humans, in their case around the muzzle, and older dogs lose their figures too. Please don't write off critters past their first flush of youth. They still have a lot of mileage in them, are loyal and affectionate, and are much better suited to retired people than a young tearaway or a puppy. Few get the chance of a home, but with kindness and a little judicious dieting they can live for years.

If you choose a pedigree or a *known* crossbreed rather than a mutt (and I am a great fan of the mongrel), do find out about the breed. Pedigree traits are fairly predictable and it's no good adopting a cross-mastiff if you are 85 and live in a flat. There are rescue dogs to suit everyone's tastes, and if you can't find a soul-mate among them, then you're very hard to please.

CHAPTER 4

Be prepared

EX-SHELTER DOGS may need a refresher course in housetraining. Battersea waifs used to go out with a message on their collars: 'Pray have a little patience with me. There are so many of us shut up together here that the keeper has no opportunity to teach us habits of cleanliness. I am quite willing to learn.'

Another difficulty for the adopted dog is a yen to trace its former owner, greatly missed. If you live close to their old haunts, you'll need to keep your adopted one on a lead or it will wander off. Give it time – it's a bit confused, that's all. The problem of wanderlust in general is much more common in males than in bitches. Males are assertive and adventurous and need firmer handling, so if you are submissive and shy yourself, you may be better off with a bitch. A male dog is rather like a poker player – he will examine you for your aces. Many police dogs have been reclaimed rejects and most are males, so you see what can be done, even with a large, potentially aggressive customer such as the German shepherd, by being firm, consistent and kind.

SEX, DRUGS AND ROCK AND ROLL

The answer to the question – 'dog or bitch?' – will also depend on which sexual habits you can put up with smilingly. Bitches have an oestrus or season twice a year, each lasting about three weeks. During this time they lose blood-stained fluid from the vagina and pester you to go out, hoping to be mated. They may, if thwarted, suffer a false pregnancy, start 'nesting' and be snappy if disturbed. They also attract local males who may congregate in your garden.

There are drugs and sprays to mask these problems, but they can be prevented once and for all by spaying. Males are not subject to 'heats' (unless they are racing dogs). Any time is right. If they sense a neighbourhood bitch in season, they become very frisky, wanting to get out. If frustrated, they may make a great escape bid, sulk, growl, mark their territory (urine stains the carpet) or make ludicrous attempts to mate with something in the house, such as a cushion or a visitor's leg. Again, such ardour can be controlled by drugs, but the vet may advise castration and if he does, please listen. Talk of neutering healthy animals may seem cruel, but consider the unwanted litter your pet may produce if he should escape – life isn't all that grand for them either, and at least your dog has a home. Vets and dog welfare workers recommend neutering because they see so many of the puppies. Of course, if you happen to have a gay dog like my late lamented mongrel Stanley, the problem doesn't arise. All that concerned *him* was the whereabouts of another mongrel called Sid.

APPEARANCE AND SIZE

Other choices such as coat-type and size are more straightforward. Long-haired luxury requires a lot of work if the coat isn't to become matted and may cause problems like runny eyes and embedded grass seeds. If you don't plan to groom your dog every day, either have it clipped or choose a smoothie. A smooth dog may moult in spring and summer, but a Mr Sheen in good condition is softer than mink and smoother than silk. A third type of coat, wiry or woolly, does not moult but needs professional clipping or stripping if you mean to keep it smart. Wiry and woolly dogs are hardy and have a certain Gaelic charm.

Size? This is really a matter of common sense. The bigger the dog, the more he will cost you to feed and the more mess he will make – of every sort – that you will have to clear up. I know of enormous dogs living happily in apartments, but they must have somewhere safe and free to run or they will feel cooped up and testy. If you fear burglars, a small dog's bark is just as effective a deterrent as a St Bernard's and consider *very* carefully before you adopt a big boisterous dog if you also have a child. The youngster won't be able to manage and there will be panic, a fight or a traffic accident. Larger dogs are very strong and can drag an adult after a cat or down the stairs (read the poem about *Brandy*).

You may weigh all the pros and cons, and then go to a shelter and come away with something completely different from what you intended. Many of us have. Don't worry about it. The dog you choose for its very awfulness will, given time, make itself beautiful in your eyes.

TEMPERAMENT

Appearance isn't everything, as every true dog lover knows. What about temperament? For some people, rescuing a dog becomes a pointless exercise unless they can save a lost soul as well – a dog who has been made completely miserable, hostile and scared by somebody else's cruelty. If you are such a person, no praise is too great, and there are enough moving testimonies in these pages from owners who have succeeded to make it worth a try. But please do it with your eyes open and don't, whatever you do, expect small children to help. Canine salvage is a delicate operation.

There are a few things you should know before you start. Firstly, most of the dogs who have ever savaged anyone have been male. Not all, but *most*. But any dog who is dominant, unpredictable, surly when reasonably chastised (*never* physically) and vengeful by nature is not to be trusted in your home. Secondly, there are very few mad mongrels, since they have not been subjected to close breeding or purpose-breeding for aggression like certain pure-breds that are known to throw volatile strains. Most behaviour problems in mongrels are not due to inherent nuttiness but to bad habits ingrained by mismanagement. Thirdly, if you take on any dog with these habits, you may be inheriting problems that led to the previous eviction of this dog, and aggression, dirtiness and noisiness are the most common. These habits are by no means impossible to eradicate, but they will take time and patience. Forewarned is forearmed. Lastly, you must not wallop the dog if he gets it wrong, or he will go backwards not forwards.

SENSIBLE PRECAUTIONS

Ask the shelter staff for details of your new dog's diet and stick to what it has been used to at first – this will avoid unduly upsetting a worried tummy. Collect the dog in the morning if you possibly can – that way it will have time to get used to your house before darkness falls and it has to sleep in a strange bed. Don't make a detour from the kennels to show your new pet to friends: come straight home. For a rescue dog the journey may be hair-raising. Have someone with you if you can, to comfort the dog as you go along.

Have everything ready at home before you arrive – its water and food bowls, its bed or box or rug, and lots of newspaper for toilet training. Have the garden fixed up: it's no good mending the fences after your bounder has bolted. Protect your pond and your prize bulbs – don't wait for the newcomer to dig them up and then give it a hiding.

And finally, please *don't* bring your rescue dog home as a Christmas present. Noisy festive seasons are not the time to be housetraining a frightened orphan. Remember, 'A dog is for life . . .'

'FEELING WITH'

Whatever rescue dog you choose, and wherever you get it from, life will be a lot easier if, at the outset, *you put yourself in the dog's place.* I know a lot of people will say *Doggerel* is full of anthropomorphism, and dogs are not human and 'don't have feelings like us'. Well, actually they do, and growing scientific evidence is emerging from studies of animal emotions. Empathy with a dog companion is not some trifling fantasy invented by sad and lonely owners. Empathy is 'feeling with'. Compassion is 'feeling with'. Sympathy is 'feeling with'. We owe it to companion animals to try to understand them. That's what these poems are all about. Once you see a dog as an individual with feelings, with signs and signals and expressions, you will begin to interpret them correctly, and you will therefore train and communicate with the dog correctly, and your reward will be abounding love and joy.

CHAPTER 5

Home from home: training

A TRIP TO A SHELTER, you may think, must be terribly depressing. Not if you intend to take a dog home. It is like being at large in a jeweller's silly sale.

The kennel staff will often know quite a bit about a dog's temperament, though some cast-offs don't take to being kennelled and behave badly because they are institutionalised. There are noisy barkers, for example, and dogs that will nip a neighbouring tail when it pokes through their netting, who when they get to the right sort of home can be restored to perfectly normal pets. Most can be rehabilitated to some extent.

Many inmates have been thrown out at the peak eviction time of around six months to a year, when pretty puppyhood ends and teething and lack of training begin to cause inconvenience. These are the doggie delinquents – no idea of discipline but leaping with enthusiasm: 'young idiots', as one rescue manager put it, 'who've been allowed to run riot.' Some of the larger charities spay all bitches old enough to have a season and castrate males on veterinary advice, although it takes six months for the hormones to change. Males may be neutered for aggression, wandering and leaping the fence. It makes the dogs more like home bodies.

GIVING THEM TIME

All rescue dogs desperately need one thing: *an owner who can give them time*. Dogs are social people. They can all learn, and as you can see from so many of our verses, they can reform. Imagine a zigzag that starts wide at one end and gradually tapers down to a simple line. This is the pattern of rehabilitation. You start with wild 'zigs' and 'zags' and gradually these swings and excesses calm down to a wavy line, steady and straight with an occasional wiggle.

Some of the rescue centres have an information sheet on each kennel, offering prospective adopters all the news they have about the waif within. One of the details given is invariably 'Reason for Re-homing', and often this box will contain three terrible words that may doom a dog: 'COULD NOT COPE'. *Please cope.*

TRAIN OR BE TRAINED

A word of advice before we get down to the nitty-gritty of homebody training. If you do not train your dog, your dog will train you. Rescue dogs are in a very high league mentally, and crossbreeds and mongrels in particular are born survivors. This means they are in a good position to do as they think fit, if you allow them to. They have strong views on doggie government and how they wish to conduct their affairs – a mentality often born of hardship. So if you bring one home, be it an adult or a puppy, you should expect to spend some time showing it the house rules. Set the tone of your relationship from the very start. If you do not assume authority, you will leave a vacuum that your rescue dog will quickly fill, particularly a male dog, accustomed to competing for all his wants.

The traditional theory of dog training or 'breaking' (note the expression) has always been based on dominance: the concept that you impose yourself on the dog as his new pack leader, to be feared and obeyed. The 'show it who's boss' philosophy has given rise to a great deal of cruelty, sticks, switches, electric shock collars, spiked chains and choke chains to physically coerce the dog into obedience.

It is perfectly possible to have authority over a dog without cruelty, and if you are dealing with an adult animal from a shelter, you have a particular responsibility to avoid brutal coercion, not only on ethical grounds but because brutal methods may force the dog into a corner from which its only recourse is savage revenge. Wolves, which sort out their internal status feuds on the alpha dominance principle, may be awfully wild and grand, but they also have horrific and fatal fights. If this is the basis on which you wish to train your dog, one or both of you may end up very badly injured. Dogs have 42 teeth, humans 32. It's up to you.

SENIOR PARTNER

The other way of training a dog is to act as senior partner, based on the principle that you know more than he does. This method is based on three rules: be firm, be fair and be kind. Put yourself in the dog's place and try to simplify things for him (or her – I use the masculine only for convenience). Remember, he's just a dog. He's not as clever as you. He may be more in tune with nature and more able with his nose and ears, but his vocabulary is very limited. Don't talk to him as if he is a member of Mensa. He won't get you. You may have to go over something repeatedly before your dog sees what you have in mind.

Be consistent – don't reward him for some momentarily amusing behaviour one minute and punish him for it the next. Be patient. A dog's greatest happiness is to be best pals with his owner and he desperately wants to live with you and not be turned out and abandoned again. Praise will always be remembered better than scolding because the latter is painful to recall. So try to engineer the dog into a position where you can praise him for something if you can, rather than moaning at him all the time. Never, ever, lose your temper. Remember these are damaged goods.

The easiest way is to return to basics. If you bring home an adult dog with some ingrained bad habit, try to work out the reason for his behaviour – what he fears and what he gains by it. Use your insight. A dog is an animal without any moral compass. He only learns what he may or may not do by your responses. These can be very puzzling. He may have been inadvertently 'rewarded' for doing what you don't want him to do. Without necessarily realising it, previous owners may have been flattered by him fearlessly protecting them and barking furiously at strangers or showing jealousy towards another family member who sits near them on the sofa. The dog may have drawn the wrong conclusions about what is required to keep humans happy. He cannot grasp threats of future reprisals, or wrongdoings of this morning being punished this afternoon. Simplify, and you will see the situation from the dog's point of view.

ASSUMING AUTHORITY

Some people have natural authority over a dog. Most do not. If you don't have this natural charisma you will have to assume it, and this will not be achieved by ranting and raving or waving your arms in the air. When crises occur, as they sometimes do, drop your voice an octave, slow down and be prepared to repeat yourself. Keep control. Keep your back straight and your arms at your sides so you present a solid shape. The late great Sir Laurence Olivier once observed that an audience respects an actor who never has to fully extend himself. Dogs know by your delivery whether you're about to bust a gasket or be master of the situation.

You are the leader of this dog. You go through the door first, not him. You go through gates and entrances first. You have your dinner first (and have a 'pretend' taste of bits of his before he is served his dish). When you come home, *ignore him.* Calmly take your coat off and go and put your things down or your shopping in the kitchen. *Then* greet the dog and make a fuss of him. This has to be the order of events in your home, because he must understand that this is your house and you are in charge of all comings and goings – not him. A rescue dog is often an *insecure* dog. Give him the stability of knowing there's somebody in charge here who will look after things and keep order. The dog then doesn't have to take charge, and in fact most don't *want* that huge burden of responsibility anyway.

Try to avoid head-to-head confrontations, big 'scenes' and battles of will. A dog can be easily diverted from a bad pattern of behaviour at the outset by simple planned tactics. One of the best diversion strategies I've seen was demonstrated to me by the country's leading authority on problem dogs, Dr Roger Mugford. This involves the use of an old coat or towel thrown on the floor, a rape alarm and a few nourishing titbits. The dog must be on the lead. At the outset of a dotty turn, the rape alarm is set off, the dog is led briskly on its lead to sit on the coat or towel and a titbit is given, followed by much praise. I've seen the method employed in Dr Mugford's surgery to great effect on biters, barkers and delinquents. A few such exercises can baffle a dog into submission and reform even the most entrenched bad habits by substituting a new pattern of behaviour.

Another very useful tip on the initial homecoming of a known 'problem' dog (and by no means all rescue dogs have these issues) comes from kennel managers at the shelters, who say the best way to rehabilitate the beastie is to keep it with you constantly, never letting it out of your sight or scent but at the same time *ignoring* it and going about your business quite normally. Let the dog see your routines and that you do not intend to harm or smother him, and he will come to you when he is ready. Only a tiny percentage of problem dogs fail to respond when they find themselves safe and sound.

CHAPTER 6

What you will need

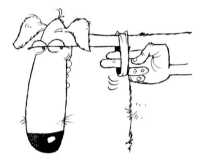

WALKIES

Your rescue dog has struck it lucky. Hundreds of thousands don't. Yours will not rake the streets or be shut in a shed, tied up, chained up or locked in a garage. Yours will be a homebody, with a collar and lead and proper walks and a bed to go to when life gets on top of him. A collar and lead are your dog's first steps to civilisation. A rolled leather or flat collar with a metal nameplate that can be engraved with your phone number is ideal. If there's no nameplate, you can attach an identity disc by the key-ring principle, though these sometimes get lost.

You may prefer to have your new pet microchipped, and this is warmly recommended by some of the major charities. Read the verse story of young Otto, who might never have ended up living in a magnificent castle, or indeed anywhere *at all*, had it not been for his Dogs' Trust microchip. In any case, a collar and identification are required by law when your dog goes out.

The lead should be of strong bridle leather or nylon, 1–2.5 metres long depending on your height, with a bolt-action trigger hook to attach to the collar. The lead should be slack as you walk. Collars are too tight if you can't get two fingers under them when they are done up, and too loose if the dog can jerk his lead out and get away. For a very small adult without much pulling power, a harness may be better. Some little dogs suffer from windpipe problems that can be aggravated by a collar.

You may also consider some training equipment to make your life easier. A Flexi-lead, which works rather like an angler's winch, unreeling and locking, or a training lead of nylon cord, 9–14 metres long with a hook collar clasp at the end, can be bought from any decent pet shop and will give you control even at a distance while your dog is learning the ropes. You could, if all else fails, attach a hook clasp to a washing line in the garden for training sessions. A little pup will need an interim 'baby' collar and lead; don't spend a lot on this as it will be quickly outgrown.

CHOKE CHAINS

Many trainers recommend the choke chain which they call, euphemistically, a 'check' chain. It works by choking the dog when it pulls and, if worn the wrong way round, can be catastrophic. Injudicious use of choke chains has caused serious injuries: neuromuscular disorders from constriction of the cervical region of the spine, ruptured windpipes, bruising to the outer and inner ears and epileptic fits triggered by constriction of the blood supply to the brain. Animal behaviourist Dr Roger Mugford researched these injuries and came up with an alternative – called the Halti – that is now widely available. See www.companyofanimals.co.uk. It consists of a simple web of straps that fits over the dog's face. It stops him from pulling by controlling his head – as a halter controls a horse. The packaging tells you how to put it on and how to get the dog used to it (there may be initial objections to the strangeness).

Unlike cat-owners, who may legally allow their animals to use other people's gardens as toilets, dog-owners are required by law to clear up after their pets. Both dogs and cats can transmit almost identical nematode parasites to the soil that may cause rare diseases in children, but only dog-fouling is a punishable offence attracting swingeing fines. Dogs have also been banned from many public areas for health and safety reasons. So I suggest (a) always carry a couple of plastic bags when you take your dog for a walk and (b) write to your MP about any injustice you may perceive.

INSURANCE

Veterinary treatment is an unavoidable expense for any dog owner, and you need to understand that health costs have recently skyrocketed, partly because animal medicine is not VAT exempt.

Many dogs currently languishing in rescue centres are there because their owners could not or would not afford veterinary treatment. The PDSA (People's Dispensary for Sick Animals), Blue Cross and RSPCA clinics rely on donations and have therefore to be judicious about which hard-up pet-owners they can help. You are therefore strongly urged to get your dog insured, and some charities, like the Retired Greyhound Trust, provide interim insurance as part of the asking price of your new dog. There are dozens of pet insurance schemes on the market so shop around. Many policies include third-party cover to protect you from liability for any damage or accident caused by your dog during its lifetime.

PREPARING YOUR HOME

What else will you need? Most vets and trainers would say an enclosed garden, please. It is possible to housetrain a dog in a flat, but it requires a lot of patience and ingenuity, use of a litter tray early on, followed by much running up and down stairs with your pet on a lead, sometimes in your dressing gown.

A garden makes all your training work so much simpler. Fences must be secure; if there is a hole in the hedge, your dog will find it. Fence off any part of the garden where the newcomer must not go and cover fish ponds with wire netting. Check to see that gates shut properly and that an amorous hound can't squeeze underneath. Unfortunately, dogs can also dig and jump. A boxer or German shepherd can scale a seven-foot fence and terriers are champion burrowers. Survey your garden carefully until you know the measure of your dog's capabilities. And please don't ever go out and leave a dog chained to a fence or post. It is very cruel.

Indoors you will need a couple of dog bowls – earthenware ones are ideal for water as they don't tip all over the floor. If you have a tall dog, bowls may be raised up by placing them on a secure stand or in suitably sized plastic bins. The water bowl must always be available *where your dog can reach it*. The second bowl is for food – better than a plate because doggie noses push food over the edge and make a mess. Wash both regularly and thoroughly. A safe dog-chewable toy, such as a big cowhide bone, will provide a useful distraction from the furniture when you go out: 'Kong' toys (ask at the pet shop) can be stuffed with food that will take the dog a good while to get at.

DIET

I strongly recommend that you stick to the food that your dog has been given at the shelter, at least initially, as sudden changes in diet can play havoc with dogs' tums. After that you can choose from the vast variety of dog diets out there, but please read the labels and follow the feeding guidelines for your dog's weight. If you choose dry food, either soak it in gravy or provide water beside the bowl (*you* try swallowing a lot of un-moistened kibble and see how you like it). Ideally feed the dog a moist food with a mixer, so he gets the best of both worlds. The packaging will give instructions on the correct proportions. Always consider paying a little extra for natural ingredients, rather than settling for animal derivatives off the abattoir floor. Finally, your own mealtime leftovers are *not* an appropriate diet for your dog. Some human foods can give him dandruff and nutrient deficiencies. Some can make him enormously fat. And some, like onions or chocolate, can actually poison him.

BEDTIME

Finally, your dog will need a bed. For a little needle-toothed pup, always chewing, a cardboard box with an entrance cut out of one side and an old blanket or sweater is quite adequate. For an adult, pet shops and suppliers offer a huge range of options from rigid plastic ones that you can line with blankets and scrub out to fibreglass ones with gentle warming panels in the base, to soft and luxurious stuffed beds and bean-beds (for the dog that can keep his teeth to himself), and expensive orthopaedic beds that make older, creakier dogs comfy. For a giant breed you could even use a folded single duvet that you can periodically stick in the washing machine.

Whichever you choose, place the bed in a corner away from draughts and paddling feet. This will be your dog's refuge, and please allow him privacy in it – all dogs sleep during part of the day. The bed of an adult should be big enough for him to turn round and round in before he settles.

Bringing your rescue dog home, you will probably find that bedtime is the hardest part of the day. When you turn out the light and retire, having praised the creature in its bed, there will be a short silence followed by whimpering and whining, and possibly even barking. Go downstairs and say *No!* very firmly. If it persists you can either repeat the procedure or take the dog and dog-bed to your room for a night or two, particularly if this is a puppy. When the house is no longer weird and frightening, you should find your orphan will sleep anywhere in it, and not mind at all.

Outside kennels are not to be recommended for a companion animal intended to share your life, and some dogs' homes specifically ask you to keep their adoptees indoors. If a dog is not good enough to live in your house, perhaps it is not good enough for you altogether, and a lot of dogs from shelters have spent quite enough time stuck out in all weathers, thank you very much.

CHAPTER 7

The first day

Don't expect too much; keep the proceedings low key. Show your newcomer his bed and bowls. Don't be surprised if there is no appetite at homecoming. Canine stomachs are queasy in a crisis and this is a crisis, for your rescue dog if not for you. He thinks: 'Oh no, I've been farmed out to some more people now, and these will get rid of me tomorrow. Nobody wants a poor cast-off dog.'

Be kind and gentle. Take several opportunities to say what a good dog he is. Imagine how you'd feel. Try to resist bunging a dogs-home waif into a bath of hot water or hosing him down in the garden on the very first day, unless you have brought home a very amenable personality. Let the shockwaves roll over him rather gradually. Show him the garden and say, 'Look what you've got!' As you can see from some of our versified stories, he may never have seen grass or flowers before, let alone a tree. Memories of past thrashings will begin to fade. You may even discern a little wag struggling to express itself, though wags may be slow in coming.

Please try to ensure that you're about the house all day on this special occasion, and avoid distressing the newcomer further by leaving him alone. Think of this as your new dog's birthday and take the day off work! Introduce the family without tumult or fuss, and be sure to let the orphan sleep as much as he wants. Sleep knits up the ravelled sleeve of care.

A NAME

Choose a name for your dog and stick to it, because this is a key word for your pet to learn. If he or she arrives with a name from the shelter that you can't stand, try to adapt it to something similar to avoid confusion. You don't have to call your dog Fido or Sandy. Use your imagination. What about Wallace, Holly, Noah, Joss, Kate, Poppy, Tuffy, Dinsdale, Hattie, Ralph, Maud, Bosie, Butler, Madge, Blondie, Oswald, Peg, Baxter, Dingo, Sidney, Sunny, Mo, Stanley, Geoffrey, Star, Chip, Pip, Oliver, Albert, Flower, Johnson, Moll, Harriet, or Daisy Dumpling?

TOILET TRAINING

You should begin toilet training on Day One. Pups are little orphans – orphan wetting and orphan messing. They sleep a lot and have frequent meals, and a puppy under three months has no more control over rear-end mysteries than a human baby. When it wakes up and after meals, or when it shows signs of wanting to relieve itself (urgent scratching, circling or squatting), pick the pup up, put it down gently in the garden and when it wets or defecates say 'Garden!' and praise it lavishly. It will then associate the word 'garden' with the toilet, and with much patience you can trigger the bodily function by using the sound, in the same way that Pavlov caused dogs to salivate to the sound of bells and tuning forks. 'Garden' is where your dog's natural functions will cause the least offence to the fastidious British public.

Indoors at night you will need some newspaper. A pup will not usually soil his own bed and will prefer newspaper to a cold floor. Over a period of time, move the newspaper zone nearer and nearer the back door until finally, as the puppy watches, you place it just outside. This will make the 'Garden' transition easier for it to understand, and eventually you'll find the creature at the back door when nature calls. Do let it out promptly, even if you're busy, or you may have to go back to square one. There may be errors. Clean them up with a little disinfectant and spray the spot with a deodoriser.

House-training may take several weeks. Scold the dog when it makes a mistake, putting it immediately in the garden, but never rub its nose in the puddle. To an animal with such highly developed scenting equipment this is very cruel. If you catch the miscreant in the very act, noise is the best rebuff. Slap a newspaper in your hand or bang an old tin tray. Don't punish the dog for an 'old' puddle. He has no knowledge of history and will think he is being scolded for his present behaviour – which may be greeting you when you come home. Remember, dogs learn by association, not 'morals'.

A dogs' home adult waif that has not been house-trained at all is less common than one that has lapsed through being shut in kennels. In any case, you should use exactly the same methods as for a pup and persevere: 'Garden' first thing in the morning, last thing at night and after meals. Lavish praise when it does its stuff, repeating the word 'garden' till it sounds to you like gobbledegook. Have patience: don't lecture the dog, and don't blame him for incompetence. One sound, however monotonous to you, is easier for him to remember: the Guide Dog Association use the word 'busy'.

An adult rescue dog may have no idea of bowel or bladder control. He may take a long time to get his degree in potty science, just like a puppy, and an adult male's problem is compounded by the fact that he cocks his leg against the vertical to trigger urination, which if he is shut indoors means one of your walls or a piece of furniture. If you have particular problems like this the vet may be able to help, as there are drugs to suppress male hormone marking in the house. Otherwise try the simple expedient of putting the dog's bed in a room with a tiled or linoleum surface and newspaper, as for puppies, and restricting the area at night by means of a 'pen'. Feed the dog at regular times and it will generally defecate at regular times. Avoid feeding him late at night. Flat-dwellers with either a pup or an adult will need a cat-litter tray, again moved gradually nearer the door.

SPRAYING

There is another sort of toilet problem – spraying. Some dogs and some bitches 'spray' when they are very excited, such as when they are thrilled you have come home. Don't smack the dog – it can't help it, and it may have been trying to control itself with a full bladder. Take it into the garden for now, and consult your veterinary surgeon.

Finally, when you are walking your dog in public places, remember to clear up after him with a plastic bag and dispose of it in a bin. Please don't risk that fine and disgrace the rest of us. We have enough trouble with bans as it is.

CHAPTER 8

Obedience

As you can see from some of the verse stories, rescue dogs are perfectly capable of a high level of obedience. The Hearing Dogs for the Deaf charity, requiring very rigorous training, began with rescue dog recruits, and many wonderful police dogs were previously turned out by their former owners for delinquency.

For most owners who don't need this level of obedience, it is sufficient to aim for a pet that obeys the law and the house rules and comes when called. There are hundreds of training clubs in Britain whose addresses can be obtained from the Kennel Club. These clubs generally accept any dog, mongrel or pedigree, over six months of age, though if you adopt a puppy you should be teaching it the rudiments beforehand yourself, not letting him run wild. Go along to a club and have a look. If you see dogs being literally throttled with choke chains or, worse still, being beaten and teased by people in padded sleeves, think very carefully indeed about enrolling your friend, especially if you think he or she may have been ill-treated. I have heard of tragic cases of dogs that have become savage after physical coercion training. Classes of the right sort can be an invaluable help. What they do is to school the owner in basic confidence at dog-handling so you can go away and train the dog yourself.

TEACHING THE BASICS

The first requirement of all obedience training is to get your dog used to the collar and lead. Pup or adult: it makes no difference. It must get used to this equipment to live in our overcrowded country and it is an offence to walk a dog along a designated highway *without* a collar, identification tag and lead. If you adopt an adult, it may well have worn them before. A puppy will find it all very strange. Put the collar on in the house for brief periods for a few days and go about your business. Ignore the rebellion: he will soon get used to it provided the collar is not too tight (two-finger room). Mother hippos train their babies to swim by knocking them off the bank and letting them get on with it and, by and large, animals make less fussy parents than we do. That's the first lesson. All the other lessons are based on the principle:

Demonstrate, Repeat, Reward

The worst enemy of anyone trying to train a dog is confusion, so be clear at every stage. Have one person teaching the dog, not half a dozen. Use few words and simple sounds that will make the association in the dog's mind, then lots of praise because rescue dogs may not have heard very much of that in this world.

'NO'

You can usually stop a dog in *flagrante delicto* by making a loud noise. Say 'No! *No!* loudly and harshly, dropping the pitch of your voice if you can. A metal tray banged against the wall makes a good accompaniment, which is very mysterious and alarming to an unruly dog (don't do this, of course, if you've adopted a very nervous critter). When he associates the act with the racket, he will desist. Smacking, on the other hand, is generally *in*effective. A rescue dog will simply associate this with past cruelty, which didn't in any case reform its behaviour to the owner's satisfaction, but instead made the dog mistrustful and scared. Let repetition and patience be your watchwords.

GETTING USED TO THE LEAD

Most of the larger dog charities walk the dogs in their shelters and therefore get them used to collars and leads. But a few of the smaller, ramshackle ones do not. Collar and lead work is a vital teaching aid. A quick jerk on the lead is an effective form of training – better than smacks, sticks or rolled-up newspapers, all of which keep the dog out of range and repel it from you. Training requires close contact, and there is no point in ordering a dog to do something if you're not in a position to enforce it. The lead is your hotline to the dog's brain.

Get a youngster used to wearing one by clipping it gently to his collar in the house and letting him run up and down under your supervision – keep an eye on him as the lead may catch on something. Chewing can be deterred by dabbing lemon juice on the leather. The next step is to hold the lead at arm's length, backing away and proffering a titbit, which will introduce the queer (to the dog) 'lead feeling' without wrenching the animal up and down. Keep the lessons short and sweet. An adult unused to a lead may be introduced in the same way, but have his lessons in the garden where he can buck without breaking anything. Don't be exasperated because you think these are rudimentary 'puppy' lessons for a grown dog. It may be completely new to him.

The alternative to a choke chain, Dr Roger Mugford's Halti, comes with fitting and teaching instructions and is worn round the dog's head like a halter with the lead attached. This, too, takes some getting used to and should be tried out in the garden, with the dog running up and down on the lead until he forgets his indignation. There is also a leather slip collar, available from most good pet shops, that will control a big dog more kindly than a choke chain if you are really stuck.

HEEL

Stand your dog on your left, lead in your right hand across your body. Hustle the dog firmly up and down, talking to him merrily. If he won't budge, use a titbit as an interim measure (but don't go mad with titbits or you'll have a fat dog). If he pulls ahead, which is much more likely, give a jerk on his collar and say 'Heel!' There's no need to wrench the dog over in a backward somersault; you'll find that if you walk briskly and make a lot of right turns, you'll automatically be in the driving seat and he'll have to pay attention to your movements. These should be short lessons, but you may have to repeat them over and over again because it's quite hard for a rescue dog to understand that he must now keep pace with a human. Some mongrels can never be bothered with precision heel work because they get bored, but so long as you can train the dog not to drag you to destruction, you have achieved the main object of the exercise.

SIT

Even the most dominant, unreclaimed adult relies on you for his food, and you should use this to demonstrate your authority. At mealtimes, hold the dog's bowl in one hand above his nose and command him to 'Sit!' Say it as though you mean it. If you have him backing away with his rear end against a wall, he will feel physically inclined to sit down anyway; otherwise use your free hand to show him what you mean, pressing down firmly on his hindquarters near the tail. No sit, no din-dins. Be firm. The food method of teaching the 'sit' is better than the lead method, pulling the dog's head up, because it offers a real reward. Pups will be fed three or four times a day, so you will have plenty of practice at instilling your authority.

STAY

This is a continuation of the 'sit', reinforced with a hand signal. If the dog gets up, make him sit down again and say 'Sit – stay!' very firmly. This is not 'teasing' the dog but capturing his entire attention at the moment when you have the most natural control over him – as his dinner-giver. It establishes in his mind that you are the giver of good things and must be listened to, and if you make it a daily routine, the dog will begin to obey you in other ways.

DOGS LEFT ALONE

Many dogs start barking and gnawing when left on their own, and some dogs that have ended up in shelters have been evicted by their owners for this very reason. A dog should be perfectly all right on his own for three or four hours while you go out, provided he has water to drink and a big cowhide bone or Kong toy to chew – and so long as you have taken a tiny bit of trouble over his training.

The method is simple. After he has gone to the toilet, calmly put the dog or pup in another room and shut the door. Go about your business, but listen for sounds of showing off or destruction. If there's a racket, bang loudly on the door and shout 'Ugh! Bad dog!' and if necessary make a great show of thundering in the room and shaming the treachery. The first lesson might last five minutes, the next ten, and so on. Work up gradually until you can leave the animal on his own for a couple of hours with complete confidence. This is training without tears, because the dog will resign himself to your absence and very probably go to sleep.

As a general rule, *over*-attachment and possessiveness will inevitably cause problems in an owner's relationship with a dog, so love him devotedly but try not to become a clinging couple. Clinging dogs make their own lives a misery and feel so lonely when left that they will defecate, drink out of the toilet bowl, tear, gnaw and howl to show you their feelings. Avoid such habits by the behind-closed door technique. If you can't face the discipline involved, consider a budgie. Dogs are like us: they express their worries in bad ways.

DOWN – STAY
Once your dog has learned to 'sit' and 'stay' for his dinner, he will sit on command on the lead and he will know that 'stay' means to keep still. If you wish to extend his repertoire, you can now teach him 'down', which is fairly easy. From the sit position, casually pull his forelegs from under him so that he is lying instead of sitting,

and say 'Down – stay!' Repeat it a few times – he may keep getting up, so be lavish with your praise when he obeys you. Reinforce the 'stay' by attaching a Flexi-lead or training cord to your dog's collar and backing away with your palm extended, increasing the distance little by little and returning to praise him profusely if he remains down. Once you're sure he's steady, you can throw caution to the wind and try it without any lead at all, but in the garden or an enclosed space at first in case he's crafty.

COME

In this lesson, rather than you returning to the dog, your dog comes to you. Have him on the long lead, walk away from him quietly and when you reach the extent of the lead, turn and face him. Call his name, say 'Come!' in a delighted, cheerful voice, and give a friendly tug on the lead if he needs any encouragement. When he reaches you, praise him a good deal because this is a wonderful thing for a dog to learn. Always bend down to praise him – don't let him jump up, not even a little puppy. Jumping can injure children and elderly people and the habit usually sets in because the dog has been encouraged to leap into someone's arms as a pup. Forewarned is forearmed.

You should practise 'come', 'down' and 'stay' many times on the extended lead before you practise without it, or free. The 'come' requires great patience, and lessons should always take place well away from traffic or livestock. If the dog takes ages to come to you, don't smack or scold him when he finally obeys. This will make the association in the dog's mind of 'come – wallop' instead of 'come – glad'. The usual response to a refusal to come should not be to chase the dog or try to stalk up on it, but to turn on your heels and start to walk away, if necessary with a titbit.

That's more or less the Green Cross Code for rescue dogs. If you are more ambitious, try kindly classes, but you can do a good deal at home by remembering that the dog is dependent on you for food, shelter and affection. As Dr Roger Mugford teaches his clients, attachment can be manipulated to your own and your pet's advantage. Owners with problem dogs frequently find it strange when they are told that often doing nothing is just as effective as doing *something*. This is why, when your dog refuses to come, the best method is not to go hounding after it, but to start walking away. And why, when you come home, you establish your authority in his mind by not making a fuss of him until he is calm. A dog's need to be loved is greater than its fear of chastisement. Diversion is better than whacking. Holding the food bowl in the air is better than a confrontation of wills. You have the greatest conceivable advantage over your dog – your brain. You don't need to go fifteen rounds with him.

CHAPTER 9

Behaviour beyond bearing

Most rescue dogs are not warmongers but peace-loving animals that have simply lost their homes. Many have come into the shelters through no fault of their own, because their owners have split up, or died, or gone into sheltered housing. But some sadly have been frightened, and some have been cruelly abused. These dogs will need the gift of time to put the past behind them and regain their trust.

Many of the dogs featured in this collection have been rehabilitated from a very bad start and turned into loving and friendly pets (retaining natural naughtiness where possible). So it can be done, and you can do it. But you need to understand 'where the dog is coming from'.

AGGRESSION

Adopted dogs, because they come to regard their owners as saviours rather than just good friends, are prone to aggressive loyalty and jealousy. Usually this causes few problems, other than to make their owners rather conceited. However, sometimes this possessiveness causes belligerent behaviour towards other animals and other people. In this case, it always helps to lower the temperature of your relationship with the dog and share it with friends and neighbours willing to lend a hand. Very often jealous behaviour has been secretly encouraged by the owner, who finds it rather flattering at first.

Don't hug the animal to you every time someone approaches or enters the room. Encourage it to have friendly exchanges with others. Show it that the world will not actually end if you leave it alone for half an hour. Don't create a 'can't cope' dog, and don't become a desperate couple. If your adopted one sees another dog while out on the lead, don't drag it away down the road as though it were a psychopath. If it barks at the 'rival', wait it out, talking soothingly until it shuts up. Let it meet its own kind. Otherwise it may form the impression 'four legs bad, two legs good'. Its behaviour may well be motivated by a desire to protect you and if it thinks you are alarmed, this will confirm its suspicions that you are indeed in danger. Stay calm and friendly.

If you are one of the unlucky few and you find your adopted dog behaving unpleasantly, examine your relationship to see if you have been somehow condoning its antics by your devotion. Your dog's status in the house should be at the bottom of the family pack, beneath your children. Most dogs accept this without much ado because, in the wild, cubs assume the rank of their parents and in wolf packs they are generally born to an august female sired by a leading male. If your dog is unfriendly towards your children, then you must get expert advice. Ask your vet to refer you to an animal behaviourist like Dr Mugford. The best behaviourists have a very high rate of success with healthy dogs that might otherwise be put down for bad conduct. A dog that is aggressive through jealousy and sees a member of your family as a rival for your affections may be helped by having the resented person attending to his feeding and exercise instead of you. A treatment plan of this kind, under expert supervision, can often save the day.

DOG EAT DOG

Status disputes between two *dogs* in the same household can generally be helped by the ruse of favouring the aggressor rather than protecting the underdog. Try it and see. The dogs would have already worked out their mutual status to their own satisfaction by means of dog signs and signals between themselves, and if you try to turn this upside down you will not prevent fights but cause them. Greet the leading dog first, and then the poor little soul to whom your heart goes out. Put the leading dog's lead on first; give him his dinner first. Don't make waves.

There are, in fact, several different types of aggression in dogs, quite apart from the possessive sort, and treatment depends on the cause. The behaviour may have been training-induced, by someone deliberately teasing the dog. It may be pain-induced due to injury or illness, in which case you may need to apply a soft bandage muzzle while the dog is being treated. It may be fear-induced, a not uncommon cause of aggression in problem dogs. The solution is not to rain blows on the animal's head, but to calm its fears, give it a sense of security and gradually desensitise it to the source of terror.

SEXUAL AND TERRITORIAL AGGRESSION

The other common types of aggression are sexual and territorial, the same as with humans. The first may be overcome by neutering – this is *always* preferable to euthanasia or abandonment. The second, territoriality, may be evidenced by the dog causing havoc over intruders such as the gas meter reader or Auntie May. Unfortunately this kind of aggression tends to become reinforced by the fact that many callers, like the postman, go away again rather quickly and the dog thinks this is because he has seen them off. There is really no solution to this kind of 'doorbell behaviour'; indeed you may be very glad of it if you live in a neighbourhood where half the passers-by are casing the joint. Just don't allow your dog to attack legitimate delivery people in the garden.

Dogs who are aggressive towards visitors in the house are usually those who dominate their owners anyway. The animal is simply taking responsibility as housemaster, assuming that his owner is incompetent in these matters. As already mentioned, dogs do not generally enjoy this responsibility. They would much prefer to live in a secure environment with a reliable leader in charge, and they only step in to fill a vacuum. Territorial aggression is therefore often a matter of assuming your natural authority over the dog. Otherwise try shutting the dog in a 'naughty room' at the first sign of bossy behaviour towards a visitor, until he is contrite. After a period in the cooler, he may be very glad of Auntie May's company.

PREY-CHASING

Dogs will instinctively chase that which flees from them – cats, hares, mechanical hares, sheep, fowl, bicycles and even cars. The *movement away* seems to trigger the dog's predatory mechanisms, and a fleeing cat may well be chased whereas a calm, seated cat will often be ignored. This is why even dogs accustomed to cats in the house will frequently chase the same sort of animal in the street or in the garden with unreasoning fervour. Cats are usually quite efficient at escaping, and some will stand at bay and give the dog a taste of their claws to teach him a lesson, but livestock are often not so lucky.

I have come across all kinds of 'cures' for livestock-worrying, from shutting the dog in a ram pen to tying a dead chicken to his tail. Obviously, fairly desperate measures are called for if your dog lives in the country and longs to kill sheep and poultry. Many lambs have been mauled by marauding dogs and if yours is caught in the act, he may legally be shot by an irate farmer. The best insight I know into the subject comes from the German war-dog trainer, Konrad Most, who was admittedly rather cruel in his methods. However, observe his reasoning. He says that if a dog is to be prevented from killing a chicken, *the correction must be given at the time when the dog has the intention of doing so.* Loud noise, a water-pistol, a citronella spray (which can be incorporated in a dog's collar – ask at the pet shop), a can of stones thrown down noisily *beside* the dog's head –

all these unpleasant stimuli can be associated in the dog's mind with the close proximity of a chicken *before* the dog has actually attacked the chicken.

You may adapt this method, without using corporal punishment, for cats, sheep or any other creature liable to be killed by your adopted dog, by showing him the animal at close quarters while he is on the lead and chastising him very severely before he has murdered anything. If you live near a farm, there may be a sympathetic farmer only too keen to give you a hand in this worthy cause.

GREYHOUND – CALMING

Greyhounds are a special case in point. Some racing dogs are trained using extremely cruel and (to the dog) memorable methods to chase rabbits and hares. Lack of enthusiasm for the task may well result in extreme punishment, abandonment or death. Greyhounds can be successfully rehabilitated and taught not to chase, and a good many go on to live quite happily in homes with cats (and even share their beds). But chasers *must* be re-trained, and this requires understanding and patience. The Retired Greyhound Trust are the acknowledged experts in this field, and will offer advice on which of their dogs are safe with cats and other small animals, and what methods to use to re-train the others. Tens of thousands of ex-racing greyhounds have been re-homed and calmed down from the job they used to do, and they make beloved and gentle family pets.

DESTRUCTION AND DIGGING

Digging in the garden is perfectly natural in dogs; in the wild they are whelped underground and bitches have long racial memories of den-digging. Bone burial is another relic of the canine past. Either fence off the flowerbeds or resign yourself. It can't be 'cured'. Destruction in the house, though, is rather different, and it usually occurs for one of two reasons: boredom associated with lack of exercise, or desperation and distress at being left alone in the house. Obviously, the first is remedied by more exercise. The best answer to the latter is 'alone' training, described earlier. Milder forms of the disease can usually be helped by leaving the radio on when you go out, and 'barking-to-absent-friends' can sometimes be stopped by judicious use of a water-pistol. Go out of the front door and listen. If barking ensues, rush back in and give the dog a good squirt.

BIN-BAG RAKING AND WHINING

Some rescue dogs are inveterate scavengers because they have had to feed themselves to survive. If they are allowed to go out unattended they will go through garbage quite shamelessly – bitches as well as dogs. The answer is simple. Don't let your dog out without you. If he whines up a storm after reasonable exercise, get very cross indeed. Tell him that if you have any more of his nonsense you'll take him to the vet's to be *attended* to in the undercarriage department. Then ignore him altogether. When he sees he can't attract your attention by showing off, he will desist.

MUCK-ROLLING

Some rescue dogs are fervent ordure-rollers, dropping their shoulders to many offensive substances in fields and forests and emerging with unspeakable stink-coats. I have no idea how to cure this, but may I suggest a plastic mac?

CHAPTER 10

Dogs most abandoned

BRITAIN'S
MOST ABANDONED
BREED

THE MONGREL

When I began writing dog books years ago, the most abandoned breed was not a 'breed' at all. The mongrel was the traditional working-class dog, and thousands of them roamed the streets before there was any legislation to prevent them, meeting and mating with other mongrels or any 'pure-bred' dog who happened to feel available.

Mongrels were therefore very numerous and very cheap, and many were regarded as canine riffraff, easily obtained and even more easily disposed of. Shelters up and down the country were full of them, despite the fact that mongrels are among the most intelligent, individual, resourceful and talented animals on earth. One of my own dog books *The Mongrel* (Popular Dogs, 1985) detailed some of their history and numerous unsuccessful attempts, such as London's annual Dog Whipping Day and a scheme by Victorian show judge Major Harding Cox, to wipe out 'the gamin of the gutter' altogether.

Many of us who have had the honour of owning a mongrel have become their standard-bearers, and I was proud to be one of the original organisers of the National Mongrel Show *Scruffts* – the non-pedigree equivalent of Crufts – that was held for many years at Hewitts Farm near Orpington in Kent. Our hundreds of contestants, competing for such prestigious titles as Best Bone Finder and Best Lamp-post User, came from as far away as Wales and Scotland, and owners were as proud of their dogs as any Crufts winner. We received a great deal of positive publicity and the whole thing snowballed. In the end we had to ask competing television crews not to interfere in the rings, and the show became so unwieldy that we asked the RSPCA to take it over as a fund-raising event.

In Britain's shelters today there are still a good many mongrels (the progeny of other mongrels) and crossbreeds (with at least one known pedigree parent and not just a passing resemblance to a particular breed), and some of our featured Doggerel dogs are of this esteemed type. But times have changed. If you ask animal welfare people these days what are the most abandoned breeds, you get different answers. There are regional variations: in Wales, for example, the most abandoned breed is probably the Border Collie. Elsewhere, two breeds vie for the title of Britain's Biggest Castaway. They are, for very different reasons, the Greyhound and the Staffie.

THE GREYHOUND

A good number of our Doggerel dogs, you will have noticed, are greyhounds. The main reason is that greyhounds are one of the most abandoned breeds, and there are thousands of them in desperate need of homes. They are over-bred and readily disposed of, and many come from Ireland with green identity numbers tattooed in their ears that you can look up on the internet to discover the dog's history and racing success.

The Retired Greyhound Trust say they are 'in the midst of a homing crisis, with more than 1,000 greyhounds in kennels and nowhere for them to go.' Another 1,000 have recently 'retired' and are waiting for a space in the kennels. Last year the RGT re-homed a record 4,700 dogs but by autumn this year, because of the recession, they were 'already 25% down on homings', which is a huge worry to the charity.

The second reason why these graceful, beautiful dogs feature a lot in this collection is that I have an ex-racing greyhound myself. His name is Jo, and as you can see from his poem and picture, he is a unique boy. My friends Cindy and Tony Hilling, who are devoted to greyhound rescue, have twelve equally loveable 'dog persons', full of hope and affection despite their cruel experiences, all living happily in their forever home and versified in this book.

Our greyhounds are treasures beyond price, worth far more to us than they ever earned by winning.

WHY RESCUE A GREYHOUND?
By **Ivor Stocker**, *Executive Director, The Retired Greyhound Trust*

A greyhound is a trusty companion, a loving animal, a loyal friend and a fantastic pet. Greyhounds are usually around three to four years old when it is time for them to retire from the track and find a new home. When they do move in with their new relatives, they settle in well and quickly become part of the family.

After finishing on the track, they undergo a remarkable transformation. They change from being the fastest breed of dog to 'couch potatoes' that love lolling around and sleeping in comfy places. Despite their well-deserved reputation as formidable athletes, they do not need lots of exercise and are easy to look after. The vast majority of greyhounds are perfectly content with two 20-minute walks a day.

Greyhounds find homes with all sorts of different people. They are loyal companions, so often make the perfect pal for elderly couples or older people who are alone. Most greyhounds get on brilliantly with children, so many find new homes with young families. Contrary to popular belief, most greyhounds also get on extremely well with cats and many can be found sharing homes with cats and other dogs.

Greyhounds are a pedigree breed and normally stay fit and healthy into their teenage years. They come in a variety of colours – black, white, brindle, blue and fawn. Greyhound coats are short and smooth, so they don't get too dirty and can come back from muddy walks relatively clean.

The Retired Greyhound Trust has 72 branches around the country [listed in Chapter 2] working tirelessly to find homes for retired greyhounds. The charity has homed more than 50,000 dogs since it was founded in 1975. For further information on adopting a retired greyhound as a pet, please contact the Trust on 0844 826 8424 or log on to www.retiredgreyhounds.co.uk.

THE STAFFIE

The Staffordshire bull terrier has for generations been one of Britain's best-loved and most popular breeds. But when vicious British yobs began to breed and train dogs on a large scale for aggression, the Dangerous Dogs Act was introduced to try to control pit bull terriers and similar *looking* breeds. Since then, Staffies have suffered a very bad press indeed.

Isolated tragic incidents in which individual dogs, cruelly trained for fighting, have attacked children and subsequently been destroyed, have been generalised to demonise the entire breed, including many thousands of perfectly innocent and harmless dogs. The British Veterinary Association and welfare organisations have pleaded for the dangerous dogs legislation – which has in any case failed to curb the breeding of pit bulls – to be reframed on the basis of what they call 'deed not breed'. In other words, attacks should be seen as the work of individual dogs rather than the fault of whole breeds. No dog should be judged and killed simply on the basis of what it *looks* like, though this is often the sole criterion in many destruction orders at the moment.

Any dog, even a pug or a Yorkie, is capable of aggression and biting. Some dogs are larger or more powerful than others and their bites can therefore be more serious. Generally speaking, if dogs are trained by mindless thugs to bite and fight, they will. But the vast majority of dogs live placidly with us, and the Staffie is no exception.

THE 'ALVIN' PERSONALITY

Staffies that have *not* been deliberately bred, goaded and trained for aggression, are loving, funny characters who make excellent family pets. 'Alvin', one of our Doggerel dogs, is a very good example of the normal Staffie personality – their main motivation in life is simply to please, protect and entertain their people. Yet these strong-willed though perfectly trainable and affectionate animals are being abandoned in their thousands by excessively safety-conscious families who 'fear the worst', even from dogs that have lived harmlessly with them for years.

Go to the average rescue shelter these days and you'll see them – Staffie after Staffie, large and small, in cage after cage and row after row, sitting there in their little pens with their miserable faces full of despair at humankind and their eyes searching you for the missing piece of this puzzle. *Why am I here? What have I done?* The sight is heartbreaking.

A recent BBC Television *Panorama* (aired on 2 August 2010) examined the crisis of dog abandonment in the UK and highlighted the plight of the Staffie. Of the 8,000 dogs Battersea received in 2009, an extraordinary 3,600 were Staffies, and this growing rate of abandonment is reflected throughout the country. Several of the dogs actually destroyed during the programme were Staffies who showed no evident aggression towards anyone.

If you have any experience at all with strong-willed breeds, please consider a Staffie for rescue. The shelter owners usually know a good deal about the dogs they house and the larger rescue organisations can help you choose a safe and suitable character for your home and even help you with his or her training.